Jon Williams & BJ Lownie

Passionate about proposals

The very best of the Pro

Strategic Proposals

Welcome to our collection!

We love working on proposals! Back in 2006, we decided to capture some of our (occasionally irreverent) perspectives on the world of bidding via a blog - 'The Proposal Guys'.

This retrospective brings together many of our favourite entries from the site. It doesn't seek to be a comprehensive guide to developing great proposals; our other book ('Proposal Essentials') will help if that's what you're after. Rather, the goal is to entertain, stimulate ideas – and sometimes to provoke. It's perhaps more a book to dip into than to read from front to back, although we'd be flattered if you did.

The articles we include reflect, roughly, the site itself: slightly more by Jon, and with weight given to the topics that have caught our imagination over the years. It's interesting to reflect on how many of the causes we've long advocated have become mainstream best practice, and how much of our terminology has entered the language of proposals. We've also added in highlights from a couple of our most popular conference keynotes and presentations over the years.

We both write in slightly different styles: the book 'speaks with one voice' in substance but not necessarily in style. "Two nations divided by a common language", as they say, with BJ in the States and Jon in the UK. But you'll find that we both bring a passion for our subject – and continuing, humble delight in being asked to work with organisations and present at conferences around the world.

Thank you for opening up this anthology. We hope you enjoy it. And we'd love to hear from you.

About the authors

BJ Lownie and Jon Williams are the principal directors of Strategic Proposals. For over 30 years, the company's helped organisations worldwide to win bids and sharpen their approach to proposal development.

BJ's background is in journalism, business operations and proposals. He's a former head of the corporate proposals group for DEC (Digital Equipment Corporation). Jon's a gamekeeper turned poacher. He started his career in procurement, before moving in 1999 to set up the Strategic Bid Centre for Compaq.

They're proud to work with a team of outstanding proposal professionals in the Strategic Proposals business worldwide. Their clients span numerous industry sectors, from IT to finance to logistics to healthcare to engineering and construction to professional services and... well, anyone who has to write proposals (and present them to clients) while seeking to win or retain business.

BJ and Jon are both Fellows of APMP, the Association of Proposal Management Professionals. They've worked with sales teams in over 40 countries, from Sydney to Stockholm to South Africa to Shanghai. They're regular, acclaimed keynote speakers at conferences worldwide, and together wrote the bestselling book 'Proposal Essentials' (available from Amazon).

Their blog, 'The Proposal Guys', was launched in 1996 after a conversation in the back of a cab in Sydney, where the duo were working at the time. Forever debating and swapping notes about proposal best practice, they decided to share their musings with a wider audience.

Contents

On: the role of the proposal

'Hurt' equals delight - Jon

Before setting off on a ridiculously early train into London this morning, I devoured a selection of the reports on the web of The Hurt Locker's Academy Award success.

When the movie came out, I'd read a glowing review of it in The New Yorker – the sort of exceptional commendation from that publication that makes something a must-see or must-read. ('Gilead', Marilynn Robinson's Pulitzer-winning novel was another such New Yorker recommendation that undoubtedly lived up to its compelling review).

I finally got to watch the movie last week on DVD and was incredibly impressed. So much so, in fact, that I'd sworn to my wife that it was a certain bet to sweep the board at the Oscars.

She, being a rational sort, pointed out that I couldn't be sure of the result, since I'd not seen the other contenders – the highly fancied Avatar, in particular. Yet I'd spent the past few days telling anyone who would listen of the film's brilliance, and its inevitable forthcoming success.

The parallels to proposals? First, think back to that New Yorker review. If the client's been successfully 'warmed up' before your document arrives, they'll doubtless approach it in a far more positive and receptive frame of mind: "I want to read this one: I've heard it's going to be great."

And then my certainty that the movie would win, even without seeing the rest of the field. True, too, for proposals – when sometimes the evaluators read a document that is so impressive that nothing else stands a chance. No matter how good the competitors' proposals, will the reader always default back to yours as 'the one that I want', looking for any reason not to choose the others?

So, what awards will your next proposal win? Best document, for sure. Best original story? Best design? Best writing? Best direction, for your work leading and inspiring the team?

Turning the Ordinary into Extraordinary - BJ

I've just finished reading 'The Starbucks Experience: 5 Principles for Turning the Ordinary Into the Extraordinary' (by Joseph A. Micelli). As the book points out, Starbucks has managed to take an ordinary cup of coffee and turn it into something much more than that. Starbucks has made a cup of coffee an experience.

Many of us have experienced the 'two shot, skinny, no foam, extra sweet, mocha caramel latte' (I think I was once with Jon when he ordered one of these). And they've created what they term 'The Third Space' (a person's home and office being the other two.)

And isn't that what our job is about? Taking something that can be pretty mundane and, dare I say, uninteresting – products, services, etc. – and finding a way to make these extremely relevant, valuable and important to the customer.

Ok, that's not some of the job – in my opinion, that IS the job.

Get over it? - Jon

I found a kindred spirit recently in a sales manager with whom I've been doing some work.

I mentioned that I'm extremely competitive. So is he.

I explained that I don't lose many opportunities on which I work. Neither does he.

I commented that I still feel frustrated by the bids I've worked on that have been lost. Him too.

Between us, we then listed the brands that we respectively boycott, having been involved in unsuccessful bids to the organisations concerned. And we realised that between us we avoid shopping in a fair percentage of high-street stores as a result.

Anyone else find that they only lose a few deals, but find it hard to forget the ones they do?!

The customer's proposal journey - Jon

- The customer will expect my organisation to win before they receive the bidders' proposals.

- When the proposal documents from different vendors sit on the meeting room table in front of the evaluators, ours will stand out from the crowd before they've even read a word of the text.

- The title page of our proposal will persuade them that ours is the document that will capture their hearts and minds.

- As they scan through the documents for the first time – flicking through the pages, their eyes alighting only on the titles and graphics – they'll be convinced that ours is going to be the best.

- By the time they've finished the Table of Contents, they'll be excited about reading the rest of the document: section titles alone will demonstrate our understanding and our differentiation.

- The Executive Summary will establish clear blue water between our approach and that of our competitors.

- The proposal Q&A (or sections in a pro-active proposal) will re-confirm our compelling story, expanding on and validating our win themes.

- Our conclusions section will ensure that they close the book with our key themes clearly in mind.

- Our proposal presentation will re-enforce their decision that we're the people with whom they want to do business.

How did you do on your last effort?

Tried by Proposals - BJ

I recently read the book 'Tried by War: Abraham Lincoln as Commander in Chief'. (McPherson, Penguin, 2008), a documentary on, as the title suggests, Lincoln as the Commander in Chief for the United States during his presidency and the Civil War (the war having begun for all intents and purposes simultaneously with him being elected President.)

One of the great many eloquent statements made by Lincoln regarding the war is:

"The political objective is the goal, war is the means of reaching it, and the means can never be considered in isolation from their purpose. Therefore, it is clear that war should never be thought of as something autonomous but always as an instrument of policy."

This statement is equally true for proposals as they relate to the overall sales process. Written for proposals, this statement would be:

"The objective is winning the opportunity; the proposal is a key component of achieving this objective. A proposal can never be considered in isolation from the overall sales process. Therefore, the proposal should never be thought of as something autonomous but always as an instrument of the sale."

As those of us who have been 'Tried by Proposals' know well, too often a proposal is looked at as separate and unrelated to the other components of a sale – the customer's perception of the responder, previous interactions with the client, the client's view of the competition, presentations (final and others), etc.

It is critical that proposals always be tightly connected to the sales process. Anything less will reduce the impact and quality of the proposal. Failing to do this, you might get lucky and 'win a battle', but you're sure to 'lose the war.'

4

'Must win' or 'will win'? - Jon

Ever worked on a 'must win' deal?

Yep, I thought so. And what's the difference between 'must win' and 'nice to win'? Generally, in practice, often not a lot. A little more involvement (interference?) from senior executives; perhaps a few more review meetings; lots more stress; those on high taking the glory if you capture the business (and preparing to point fingers if you don't)?

I was chatting about this to a team recently, and recalled a lovely phrase used by Gerard Houllier, when he was manager of my beloved Liverpool. (That's a soccer club, for American readers).

He was asked in an interview: "Is it reasonable to say that Saturday's match is a must win game?"

His reply?

"It's not a must win game. It's a will win game."

I think bids should be like that. 'Must win' isn't good enough, if it merely means that senior folks take a little more interest and bring greater pressure to bear on the proposal team. 'Will win' implies serious commitment and support from those on high, with a corresponding focus on providing the right resources to do what's necessary to produce a first-class proposal in an efficient way.

So, next time you're told a deal's a 'must win', why not stop and ask whether it really is – or whether it's actually a 'will win', and what's going to be done to make it so.

Establishing relationships - BJ

Prior to Christmas, while in England as part of an internship sponsored by his college, my nephew Cam's laptop, an Apple MacBook, died. (OK, maybe 'was killed' is a more appropriate description as this was the result of a drink being spilled on it.).

Prior to this happening, Cam had decided that when it was time to replace this laptop, he'd probably switch to a PC.

Cam took the laptop into an Apple store and had it diagnosed. It was determined the mother board would need to be replaced and the cost would be approximately $500.

He made a call to his father, who was in Germany at the time, and they decided to have the laptop repaired rather than replacing it. The repair would only take a day or two.

When Cam returned to the shop and attempted to pay, the person helping him informed him that his credit card was declined, as the charge exceeded its limit. Somewhat embarrassed and confused, he gave this person his other 'for emergencies only' credit card. To his further embarrassment and dismay, this card was also declined (he didn't realize that the limit on this card was lower than the amount being charged as well.)

As one might expect to be the case, all this was quite upsetting and embarrassing to Cam, a young man away from home and in a country other than his own. He told the clerk he'd have to call his father, but he wasn't sure if he'd be able to reach him.

As Cam was preparing to call his father, the clerk handed him the laptop and said, "Merry Christmas. It's on Apple".

Despite having previously thought he'd switch to a PC in the future, when he posted about this incident on his blog he finished with "Apple Forever".

Now, in the future, should it happen that Cam finds himself on an evaluation team and one of the companies being considered is Apple, guess how Cam is going to view that proposal?

The decisions made by evaluators are based on much more than just the proposal itself. They also take into account, both consciously and subconsciously, their relationship, interaction and experience with the company, as well as what they've heard, read and seen.

Strategic engagement - Jon

A quick start-of-year test of how strategically you're operating. You're back from the festive break. (At least, we hope you had a break, and didn't have to work on proposals *all* the way through the holiday season).

So: do you have a clear list of the most critical deals for your sales team in the coming quarter and year as a whole, and are you already talking to the relevant salespeople about each of these opportunities?

The proposal centres who are operating strategically will already be clear on many of the most important deals in the pipeline that'll need their support. There'll be active pre-proposal planning work already underway on each deal. Looking externally, this will help the salespeople to ensure that everything possible is done before the RFP arrives to understand and shape the client's requirements. Focusing internally, this will involve preparing the proposal team for success, and gathering preliminary content.

Sadly, too many proposal centres will come back at the start of the new year simply facing a backlog of work from the holiday season, with little or no chance to lift their eyes to the horizon. If you're in this camp, why not fire a note to sales management, asking about their pipeline and requesting the chance to engage as early as possible to help them win in the year ahead?

I'm not a Bid Manager! - Jon

I've been having some lively debates lately with clients on that age-old favourite, the respective definitions and roles of bid management versus proposal management.

In case it helps others, let's go back to basics. Your organisation has a sales relationship with a current or prospective client. At some point, your salesperson will identify an opportunity to capture a piece of business in the future. You'll need to carry out a range of bid activities if you're to win this contract or project – meeting the client, conducting proofs of concept, arranging reference site visits, negotiating… as part of which, you'll doubtless submit a written proposal.

Our experience suggests that many of the problems experienced on larger deals result from confusion between the bid and proposal roles. Particularly, companies assume that their bid managers – client-facing, expert in bringing together the best technical and commercial resources to define a robust solution – are equally adept at articulating their story through the written word. And, frankly, that's rarely the case – even were the bid manager to have the necessary time available to devote to the proposal effort.

Likewise, danger lurks whenever a proposal professional lays claim to expertise outside their scope of expertise. Ask me to coach a team through the negotiation phase? Not my skill – but I know the best people to do so. Get me to review the terms and conditions, design the offer, build the pricing model – I could probably muddle through (in some market sectors), but it's not what I'm best at, what I'm paid for, or where I should be spending my time. And bidding is no place for enthusiastic amateurism.

APMP doesn't always help matters: in its drive to grow its membership base over the years (and, perhaps, to reflect the commercial aspirations of some of its sponsoring companies), it's diluted its focus away from proposal management (the clue's in the name, folks) to discuss capture planning, business development and the like. You know: if I wanted an expert in business development, I'd turn to one of the many excellent sales consultancies or forums out there (such as Huthwaite or Miller Heiman), rather than rely on a group of proposal folks seeking to broaden their horizons.

Cost of sale does play a factor, of course. I fully recognise that some organisations can't afford to engage both a bid manager and a proposal manager on a deal – just as many can't justify specialist writing, graphics or document management resource within their proposal centre. I'm nothing if not a pragmatist.

But if there's no separate bid manager, I'd advocate reallocating most of their responsibilities into the sales and technical teams, rather than inevitably compromising the quality of that so-important proposal. And the fact remains that those organisations which maximise their win rates do, by and large, clearly understand the difference between the bid and proposal, and resource their efforts accordingly.

There are winners and there are... - Jon

From a salesperson in a learning review last week:

"I don't feel that we lost it, we just didn't necessarily win it."

No. You were the incumbent. The customer came out to tender. Your main competitor now holds the contract.

You lost.

12 tips for writing proposals when you are the incumbent - Jon

1 Don't be scared to walk away. Put another way, don't feel that you have to bid. Even (especially) when you're incumbent, work out whether this is good business for you to win – and whether the deal is winnable. If you've been losing money on the contract for years, their requirements are unrealistic, they're a nightmare to work with and their chief decision-maker's best friends with a competitor, then qualifying out may be the best option.

2 Try and avoid them seeking competitive quotes in the first place. At the very least (e.g. if they're a public body which has to re-tender), think what you can do to wire the RFP in your favour – you should have the information, and the access to their people, needed to influence their requirements and criteria.

3 'Play nice' in the period up to renewal – make sure there's real focus on quality and cost-effectiveness of everything you do in the run-up to the tendering process, and try to throw in some new ideas and improvements as you go.

4 Draft your proposal well in advance. You should be able to predict the questions that they'll ask. So develop your content, review it, highlight gaps in

your knowledge – and make sure that your time between RFP receipt and the submission date can be spent on fine-tuning and tailoring.

5 Play back praise. If you've got 'nice quotes' from the customer's staff (at various levels – operational as well as senior management), or data points showing how well you're doing, use them. Actually, more than this – make sure that your pre-proposal planning discussions recognise the need for such quotes, and that the sales team (actively but subtly) goes about gathering them before the RFP arrives.

6 Be honest. If things have gone wrong in the past, acknowledge them – but show what you've learned, and what you've done differently as a result that has avoided a recurrence of the problem.

7 Use their data. If you're the incumbent, you should have detailed insights into what they do now, and into volumes, costs, service levels, timescales, etc. There's no excuse for your proposal not being the most detailed and specific, in terms of its recommendations and the way it presents the benefits of the proposed new solution.

Present your improvement suggestions. One would hope that your 'insider's view' should help you to generate good ideas as to how things could be done better.

8 Show how you've improved things over the lifetime of the contract that's coming to an end. (Sub-text: we don't only offer you cool stuff when you force our backs to the wall).

9 Subtly – reflect the cost and risk of change, should they go to an incumbent.

10 Be clear, if asked, that were you not selected, you'd handle any 'transition out' with the utmost professionalism – that the customer's ongoing success matters to you, even if you're not chosen as their supplier.

12 Remember that the competition will be hungry to dislodge you. "What would we do were we in their position?" is an important test.

Keeping it in the family? - Jon

My train-journey-neighbours have just departed – senior managers en route to a bid presentation, amazingly indiscreet, as people so often are on public transport. I've been entertained for the past two hours with a full account of their proposed solution, as they've polished up their PowerPoints and fortified themselves with free coffee.

Just before they left, the older of the two confided in his colleague: "Have I mentioned that the chair of the evaluation committee is my brother-in-law's girlfriend's dad?"

As grounds for optimism, it's not the strongest win strategy I've ever heard, but I'm guessing that the bid plan might feature him taking his wife over to see her brother for a family reunion this coming weekend!

Finishing first - Jon

The BBC website today quotes cyclist Mark Cavendish, after he had been congratulated for finishing as runner-up in a major race:

"Don't ever, ever, congratulate me on finishing second."

I rather like that, as a variant on the old quote that "silver medals were invented to make losers feel better about themselves", or legendary Liverpool soccer manager Bill Shankly's "First is first: second is nothing".

Collective experience - Jon

Some statistics from a keynote speech that BJ and I gave recently to the 200 attendees at the recent APMP UK conference:

- Over 1,000 trees had been cut down in the past year to generate the paper needed for the hard copy proposals we'd submitted: hopefully they'd all come from sustainable sources!

- We had around 1,500 years of proposal management experience.

- We'd won some £12bn ($18bn) of contracts in our careers – roughly equivalent to the Gross Domestic Product of Paraguay!

On: pre-proposal planning

Of hunters and hunting - BJ

I recently presented at a conference held by one of our clients. For this organisation, the market has shifted significantly, and they can no longer rely on the steady stream of business from existing customers they've enjoyed for many years. For this reason, the focus of their annual event was business development with an emphasis on winning new business (rather than renewals or additional business from an existing client).

Several of the presenters spoke about sales people being 'hunters' and offered suggestions for improving their 'hunting' skills. Among such tips were to start learning about the potential client as early as possible and not waiting for the RFP to arrive to get started.

The speaker's use of the terms hunter and hunting prompted me to consider the parallels between business development and deer hunting. I imagine this was also prompted by my residing on a very large piece of property that is home to many deer and the fact that this is deer hunting season.

The people who are given permission to hunt on the property fall into two groups. The first group is those hunters who have hunted the property for many years and who hunt each year for several days or weeks. This group is made up of people who live nearby and/or are close friends.

The second group consists of individuals who haven't hunted here previously and typically only hunt for one or two days. These might be clients or someone I've recently met who are hunters and who, upon learning that I have access to good property for deer hunting, request permission to hunt for a day or two.

Those hunters who haven't hunted here previously, and who only hunt occasionally, rarely see, let alone manage to shoot a deer. They might stumble upon one and take a shot at it as it runs off. They have no idea where the deer are and have no understanding of their habits. They will inevitably come in after a day of hunting to inform me there probably aren't many deer on the property anymore.

In contrast to these occasional hunters, those hunters who have hunted the land for several years know a great deal about their prey. Throughout the Spring and Summer, they are out on the property, watching the deer and learning the habits of the deer. They know where they sleep, where they eat and drink and which paths they follow. They even go so far as to put up motion-activated cameras which take pictures of the deer as they pass.

These hunters have a plan when they go out to hunt. They often have selected the deer they wish to get and will pass up deer that come by to get the one they have decided to pursue. Inevitably, these hunters get the deer they are after. They inform the herd on the property is large and there is no shortage of game for hunting.

As with most of my analogies, I think the parallels to our business are fairly obvious. The majority of opportunities are won by those companies that engage with the client well before the release of an RFP. These companies have extensive knowledge of the client and understand their concerns and their objectives for both the business overall and the RFP specifically. They know the competitive landscape and have developed their strategy for capturing the opportunity. In many cases they may have even assisted the client in the development of the RFP. (This is not dissimilar to hunters that provide food for the deer in the later part of winter to ensure the deer remain healthy when natural food becomes scarce.)

My favourite story - Jon

Browsing in the bookstore at Gatwick airport recently (ending up with Hillary Mantel's truly magnificent, prize-winning 'Wolf Hall'), I couldn't help but overhear a conversation nearby between a mother and her young child.

"This book looks really interesting," she said.

"But I want this one," he replied, pointing to another choice.

"What about this one?"

"Don't want it. I like this one." Fixed on his original choice.

"Look! This is brand new."

"But this one's my favourite story."

And at that, I had to smile. For the child had just echoed the thought process of so many potential customers when they start their evaluation process. If your sales colleagues haven't already positioned your story with those who'll read your proposal – if yours isn't already the buyers' 'favourite story' – then you're facing an uphill (and potentially unwinnable) battle.

Now, some would use this as an excuse to treat proposal staff as underlings, as administrators. But to me, it's the best argument of all as to why we proposal folks should be engaged as early as possible by our sales colleagues.

Let's Get Cooking - BJ

I often use analogies to help express ideas and concepts - and I often use the analogy of restaurants when explaining proposal support.

On a recent Saturday morning, I stopped in to say "hi" to my brother Ken and his family. My brother-in-law, David was also visiting, from Las Vegas, where he is a head chef at one of the major hotels.

Ken and his wife were having a dinner party that night, with David preparing the meal. Guests were due to arrive at 6pm and dinner, a Mexican meal with fare such as empanadas and carnitas, was planned for 7:15pm.

As we were sitting at the table finishing a late breakfast, about 11:15am or so, David looked at his watch and said, "Well, I guess I'd better get started on dinner".

What? Start preparations on a dinner some 8+ hours before it was due to be served?

When I asked him why he was starting so early, David listed all he had to do, in which it needed to be done, and how long each task would take, in order to prepare the meal. As he spoke, his experience with meal preparation was immediately obvious. It was also obvious he had a concern for preparing the best meal possible. David is as passionate about food and cooking as Jon and I are about proposals.

David pointed out that it was possible to prepare a meal in a much shorter period of time, but the quality would definitely suffer. He would have to take short cuts, wouldn't be able to pay as much attention to detail and he might even miss an ingredient or two, which had happened many times before when he rushed or hadn't had enough time. He said the time put into the preparation of a meal was always evident in the quality of the meal served.

As I listened to him, I realized the parallel to proposal development. Those groups that understand what needs to be done and allow enough time, getting started as early as possible and as needed, operate in much the same way as David does. These groups know what needs to be done. They don't cut corners and they pay attention to the details. They produce high-impact, high-quality responses and they do so in an efficient manner.

Those groups that don't get started until the RFP is released, or worse, after some time has elapsed since the RFP was released, inevitably produce a much poorer quality response – and doing so is much more difficult and stressful.

Great proposals, like great meals, require time to prepare and the way to have enough time is to, as David did for this dinner, get started well before the meal – the response – is to be served.

Let's Get Cooking – Part II - BJ

In my previous post I wrote about my brother-in-law, David, preparing a meal for a dinner party. I spoke about how he started preparations for the meal some 8+ hours before it was to be served.

As I was discussing with David and my brother Ken the parallels to proposal preparation – getting started well before the RFP was released – my brother asked, "And did you notice what David did first?"

"David began by clearing the kitchen counter, emptying the trash and checking the edge on my knives." (David hadn't brought his own knives and was using

16

Ken's, which he found to be somewhat dull. Ken brought out his knife sharpener and David sharpened each of the knives.)

We discussed this parallel to proposals. Rather than jumping into things, David took the time to prepare his work area and his tools. Having the proper tools and an appropriately set up work space allowed him to then focus on the task at hand, rather than having to repeatedly stop to find a tool or to make room to work.

It is the same with proposal development. Those who have an appropriate space in which to work and the necessary equipment and tools, are able to focus on the task at hand – and are able to work much more effectively and efficiently... resulting in higher-impact, higher-quality responses.

Little Britain: the proposal perspective - Jon

The duo behind the immensely popular comedy show, 'Little Britain', are coming to the end of an incredibly successful tour of the UK: in one year, they're apparently sold a million tickets and brought in £25m in revenues.

When the audience turn up for the show, they expect to see their favourite characters and hear their favourite punchlines.

The same applies at concerts. I've been to a couple recently (The Divine Comedy and Muse, as you ask) and it's always the group's best-known tunes that get the crowd singing along. Fans are unlikely to walk out humming that superb new track from the latest album, due out next week, if they've never heard it before.

I can see a direct analogy to the proposal world. If your audience has never heard of you, if they know nothing about your solutions, and have no idea of your story, they're unlikely to look forward to reading your document – or to find it especially memorable.

That's one of the reasons why I place so much emphasis on the pre-proposal planning phase of any proposal efforts that I work on. As a proposal manager, I should be able to expect my proposal to be sown onto fertile ground, and I'll fight for the right to harass and cajole the account manager into positioning our

17

story with the customer's decision-makers before our document lands on their desk.

A year ahead - Jon

So many proposal teams are engaged by their sales colleagues to respond to RFPs. Their skill, their energy, is deployed reactively, against the clock, at a point in the bid process where the opportunity to influence the client is already significantly diminished.

So much more rewarding to be the proposal manager I was working alongside last week. Her sales team had identified an opportunity to capture a substantial piece of business – but the RFP wouldn't be issued for a year. An initial meeting had been scheduled with the client; would she care to be involved, and could she offer any advice?

We chatted through some of the key questions they might want to ask, to understand (at a high level, at this stage) the customer's key drivers for contemplating change; their view of the ideal solution; the competitive landscape (especially, their perspectives on the incumbent); the procurement approach they were likely to follow.

We talked about the potential for proactive documents well in advance of the RFx, to try to short-circuit the process or (at least) influence the client's requirements and spec. I encouraged her to jot down key words and phrases used by the customer during the discussion: to start to live and breathe their environment. And I urged her to fade largely into the background in that first meeting – not to tread on the salesperson's toes!

By the end of the discussion, I was itching to get more involved: to work on the campaign from start to successful finish. How much better it is for proposal folks to engage with sales in this way – rather than last minute – and how much greater the value we can add!

Prepared to win? - Jon

For me, one of the most important processes in the proposal lifecycle is Pre-Proposal Planning. We coined this phrase a few years back, to capture those activities that a proposal team should undertake prior to receipt of the customer's RFP. I want to make sure that by the time that RFP arrives, our team is ready to rock and roll; that we've captured all of the necessary information about the customer's needs and our competitive landscape; that we've influenced and conditioned the customer to expect us to win.

Chatting about this with one of our team members recently, I hit on an analogy.

Imagine your favourite sporting team, about to play in the biggest game of the year. For BJ, it could be the Yankees on the eve of a World Series; for me, Liverpool coming up to a European Cup soccer final.

The coach gathers the players together, 24 hours before the big match. "I've just checked my diary, and noticed we've got a match tomorrow. Anyone free – hope no-one's planned a day out with the family? Tell you what, let's meet up in the parking lot outside the stadium – say half-an-hour before the game starts? Not sure who'll be on the team – we can have a chat about that once we get there. And don't forget to make sure your kit is washed and ironed…. Oh, and anyone read the newspapers recently? I guess we ought to check which team we're playing against."

That feels an awful lot like many proposal teams approaching a big deal. Of course, the top-notch sports team would have planned immaculately: studied the opponents in detail, trained endlessly, chosen their best team, trained, practised their tactics, organised the logistics and so on.

It should be no different for a professional proposal team! Of course, the level of preparation should be commensurate with the size of the deal. But that's no different to the sports club (where the youth side will probably go through the same routine as the top team, albeit abbreviated, and the coaches won't necessarily be quite as good).

The evaluators? Just like pussycats! - Jon

Bored at lunch the other day, I passed the time watching the gig that was showing on the large plasma screen in the corner: the Pussycat Dolls, at some recent music festival.

What particularly struck me was the make-up of the audience. Directly in front of the stage, a few rows of youngsters danced away ecstatically; behind them were ranked row upon row of seats filled with bored-looking adults.

So, picture if you will the customer's evaluation team, reviewing your proposal:

Who are the kids who'll be singing along in the front row – excited, knowing the words; the ones who were delighted to see your name appear on the festival line-up, who've been looking forward to this for weeks, who'll tell their friends how great you were?

Who are the folks who really aren't here to see your performance: they really don't like your stuff – they just wanted to get a good spot ready for their favourite band, next on stage?

Who'll be sitting, looking bored, in the corporate sponsors' seats: there on sufferance, pre-disposed to be bored, hard to win round, but potentially the ones paying for the tickets and the drinks?

Now it's not my job as a proposal manager to get in amongst the stakeholders within the customer's organisation. But I do believe I have the right to test that the salesperson will have done so by the time they get to read the proposal. And I also have the right, the need to suck the salesperson dry of information about the potential audience so that I can fine-tune my performance – proposal – accordingly.

Winning the tournament - Jon

I spent a couple of lovely days recently as chief cheerleader for a dear friend who was playing in a pretty high-powered tennis tournament. (You'll be pleased to hear that said cheerleading was of the sit-drinking-coffee whilst shouting

"Good shot!" variety, rather than involving me wearing a cute dress and waving pom-poms).

As I watched, a few parallels struck me that might be useful for us proposal folks:

1 The time devoted to preparation. The final two days of matches were played at Wimbledon. The previous five days were spent practising on grass courts. (How often do proposal teams come together for the first time after the RFP's arrived?)

2 The role of the coach. The tennis team wouldn't have dreamt of practising without bringing in a skilled coach – someone who'd help each of them to refine their technique and polish their skills. (Too often, proposal teams comprise the same old people, with no fresh faces to stimulate improvements).

3 Unsettling the competition. My friend was in no doubt from the start that she was going to win the tournament. That had a huge mental impact on the other competitors – the third-best player in the event, for example, repeatedly double-faulted on her usually reliable serve when facing my friend. (What do you do that unsettles your competitors?)

4 Confidence at every stage. Tennis players facing a serve concentrate incredibly hard – on where they're going to hit the ball, on the importance of winning the point. The moment they allow their minds to think, "Don't miss!" is the moment they do precisely that. (Your behaviour as a proposal manager impacts your team that way; confidence breeds success, and you have the power to make your contributors think of themselves as winners).

5 Every point counts. (Every question in the RFP counts, too!).

6 Celebrating success. The women's singles trophy that my friend won was almost as big as her. Her name went up onto the honours board for everyone to see, alongside the other winners dating back for 50 or so years. (Where's your proposal centre's honours board, of the bids you've helped to win? And don't forget – when people look up at the boards, there's no record of the losers).

And, of course, said friend's success was all down to my cheerleading abilities, of course!

Off to a Good Start - BJ

I was reading an article in the local newspaper today on white water rafting in which a river guide with Still River Outfitters (who operate on the Still River in Vermont), Craig Commody, discussed the dangers inherent in the activity. He emphasized the need for proper planning, being prepared and always keeping safety in mind.

He had a saying to help the people on his tours keep in mind preparedness and safety. He told them it was important to "Do the right things first and do the first things right."

This definitely applies to our work.

If you get the pre-proposal planning, the initial qualification, strategy development and the planning right, most of the rest will fall in line. And paying attention to these critical areas will certainly help prevent problems that would arise if you don't pay attention to these critical areas.

The battle ahead - Jon

I was struck by a fascinating phrase in a recent article in The Times by Colonel Richard Kemp – a former Commander of British Forces in Afghanistan. "Soldiers," he wrote, "don't begin to earn their pay until the bullets start flying."

Whilst one can see what he's trying to say, this sounds very strange indeed in the context of the modern military, where keeping the peace is just as important a role as combat operations, never mind being disrespectful to those of his colleagues whose postings at the time happen to be away from the front line.

And, much as I wouldn't for a moment try to equate what we proposal folks do with the valour of our military friends, I see a parallel in attitudes. Too many senior executives and salespeople believe that proposal professionals are best-used in the heat of the battle, under pressure, against tight deadlines. Yet so much of our value-add comes at the pre-proposal stage, doing the reconnaissance, getting the logistics in place, preparing the ground for success.

Where we really earn our pay isn't in the late nights trying to persuade the copier to work or the PDF to upload; it's in those early days where we make it far more likely that we will win the 'fight' and that we'll fight on our terms.

"No story lives unless someone wants to listen." - J.K. Rowling

On: qualification

A qualified success - Jon

The topic of qualification – the 'bid / no bid' or 'go / no go' decision – has raised its weary head in several recent conversations with clients. It's also one of the cornerstones of the APMP accreditation syllabus.

So I've put together a 'baker's dozen' thoughts on the essence of a good qualification process, in the interests of helping you test your own approach.

It's not a comprehensive list, by any means, but if you're doing all of this stuff well, your qualification process is probably in good shape.

1 Be conscious from the outset that to 'no bid' runs counter to the instincts of most salespeople. They spend their life trying to hunt out opportunities to win business; they engage the prospect in dialogue about a specific contract; they start to convey your company's appetite and capabilities for the work. And then they're expected to have to decide – admit, even – that it's not a good deal for them to pursue? This is an area that needs handling with particular sensitivity.

2 Treat every opportunity as 'qualified out until it's qualified in', rather than the other way around. For too many organisations, 'bid' ('qualified in') is the default setting – causing the proposal centre to be seen by sales as a 'business prevention' unit when debates start as to whether or not to pull the plug on the opportunity. But if your role is seen as helping the salesperson to gain support, resources and funding for their bid, you'll suddenly be 'on their side'!

3 In the words of the APMP Foundation Level exam: qualify early and certainly well before the customer's requirements document arrives. Clearly, an RFP (or the equivalent) provides a host of new information about the opportunity and the customer's specification. But by the time it arrives, you should at least have 'in principle' approval to bid, subject to certain assumptions that you've made turning out to be true once you've reviewed the RFP. And that final post-RFP-receipt endorsement of your qualification decision needs to take place rapidly after the customer's document has landed – the clock's ticking, and you don't want to sit around waiting for approval.

4 Involve the right people in the debate. Ever experienced a situation when a qualification forum has agreed on a 'no bid', only for the sales staff to escalate the debate to a more senior level and to succeed in having the decision reversed? If they're that important to your decision-making, make sure they're directly involved.

5 Make sure that if you do reach a 'go' decision, that does result in the definite and timely provision of the resources needed to chase the deal. Particularly, those involved in the qualification decision need to feel a sense of personal commitment to the outcome – if you're party to saying 'yes', there's an onus on you to make sure that your area of the business then plays its full part in making the bid a success. And if the people who control the necessary resources aren't involved in the qualification process, it can be tough to then secure their buy-in.

6 For too many organisations, qualification is merely a hurdle for the salespeople to overcome: "score 40% or more on the checklist and you can bid". Guess what? If that's the game, your typical salesperson will engineer their score to be at least 43% (allowing a small margin of error for decency's sake, and in case they get challenged on a couple of scoring criteria). Adopt what we term an 'active qualification' approach, in which you ask the salesperson not only how they're currently scoring on an issue (e.g. 'strength of relationship with the client's decision-makers'), but what that score could be by the time the customer reaches the date on which they'll make their decision – and what actions would need to be undertaken to improve their score, and hence their win probability.

7 Use simple, memorable qualification criteria. We advocate four: "Is it real, do we want it, can we win it, can we do it?" Pretty much all of the more detailed discussions you'll need to have can be categorised under one of those headings – and there's real power in having a qualification mantra that everyone involved in bidding understands and can repeat.

8 Make sure your process has teeth. It's not uncommon for me to be assured by a client during a benchmarking exercise that they do indeed have a qualification process – often a time-consuming and complex one at that. Yet when I ask what percentage of deals they qualified out of the previous year, they look blankly, and confess that it was a round number: 0.

9 Treat the usual last-gasp tactics of salespeople (we can't win, but we've got to bid because either "it's strategic" or "if we don't bid this time, we won't be invited to bid on their next deal") with healthy cynicism – even, perhaps, a degree of disdain. I've worked on bids that have fallen under those headings – but only after a particularly thorough review, and with a clear strategy as to what we're going to do in our proposal, knowing that we won't win and that doing so isn't actually our goal.

10 Be brave! Recognise that your qualification decision may change as the deal progresses – particularly, as you learn more about your competitive position. If something happens to convince you that you're wasting your time, shout about it! Even on the most reliable airlines, flying the most modern planes, sometimes people need to listen to the safety announcements so that they know where to find the emergency exits!

11 Subject to the above... make sure the client is always given a clear, consistent, early and honest view of your intent regarding whether or not you're going to expect to bid.

12 Handle any 'no bid' decision extremely sensitively. Planning, scripting and rehearsing the feedback to the customer needs great care – as does coaching salespeople in how to handle the buyer's likely objections ("but we do want you to bid: of course you can win" being shorthand for "if you drop out, you might compromise my purchasing process and / or my personal credibility internally").

13 Be clear on the role of the proposal manager in the process. Do you own the salesforce's or business unit's revenue target for the year? No? I thought not. So our role in helping those folks to achieve their goals is to offer advice from a proposal perspective (is it possible to produce an appropriate proposal in the timescales?), perhaps mixed with a sense of the deal's 'winnability' drawn from your bidding experience, perhaps blended with your ability to act as an excellent facilitator (and to be seen, perhaps, as an independent in the process, sitting 'between' the salespeople and the business). You have the right not to be expected to waste your time on lost causes. And yes, you may sometimes have to be the one that provokes the telling debate – given (1) above, salespeople are rarely the first people to jump up and say: "you know what – we shouldn't go after this". But, ultimately, it's not your call.

"It's strategic!" - Jon

When the answers to the four questions that make up the qualification mantra – "Is it real, do we want it, can we win it, can we do it?" – are "no", salespeople often resort to an alternative attempt to justify proceeding with the bid...

"But it's strategic!"

What does that mean in practice? Typically, they're stating that – to paraphrase Baron de Coubertin – it's the taking part that matters, not the winning. I can think of five potential scenarios to justify an "it's strategic" bid – one where a rational evaluation of the usual questions would otherwise cause you to down tools:

1 Known future opportunity. We can't meet the customer's requirements or we know they won't choose us. However, we can demonstrate that losing this – but doing so extremely professionally – will help us to capture a specific, known future piece of business with this customer.

Before heading down this route, be clear on what that future opportunity is and when it's happening – specifics here, not "we think they'll have stuff for us at some point". And do a careful analysis of how this tactic will enhance your reputation with the client. The pros come potentially from the opportunities that arise to develop relationships through face-to-face bid discussions, from showing you can develop high-quality proposals and (potentially) from conditioning the client's views / requirements for that future deal. The cons are that being branded 'unrealistic' or 'losers' isn't always a positive place to be.

2 Recovering credibility. Previous bid engagements with the client concerned have been a disaster. They think we're unprofessional, inept, and don't think we see them as an important client. They've extended an olive branch to us – and if we 'no bid' this time, or bid badly, we'll never be invited back.

Submitting and presenting an excellent proposal is part of a clear, wider plan to restore our reputation and re-establish positive personal connections with their decision-makers. We can't meet their requirements this time, however, but we can share experience and insights that will help their project to succeed, and could potentially offer a non-compliant solution as a 'fallback' option should their 'plan A' fail.

3 Market penetration. We have a new product, service or solution; perhaps we're in a new country or new sector; maybe we've built up a relationship with an entirely new customer. We need to be seen as 'players' and hence taking part – even if we don't win – is key to building relationships and establishing our brand in the new area.

And we're still in stages one or two of the three-stage journey in customers' inevitable progression from viewing us as "new, interesting and creative" to "we know they're serious contenders in this market" to "they've been trying for ages and they never win – they're risky".

4 Competitive attack. We know we can't win, but we're not prepared to let competitors (and especially the incumbent) have a clear run at this. We're going to bid, potentially at very low prices, to unsettle our competitors and (potentially) stop them making excessive profits from the deal – despite the risk that they'll then do the same to us, and margins in the market as a whole will end up being degraded.

5 Desperation. The salesperson can't answer "yes" to each of the four key qualification questions, but believes there's a pot of gold at the end of every rainbow. There's not much else in his/her pipeline ("I've not got anything better to do"), and they need to show that they're busy. He/she would love to bid, as miracles do sometimes happen – particularly, if bidding comes at little or no personal cost (in other words, other people will do all of the hard work!).

Of these, four tactics may potentially be viable justifications – provided it's agreed clearly, in advance, that 'losing well' is the goal – and that the bid / proposal strategies reflect this.

The fifth, and the one that seems to be most prevalent, certainly isn't an acceptable justification for proceeding with a bid – taking effort and energy away from other deals with a more realistic chance of success.

Try forcing the salesperson to explain which of the other four scenarios their deal fits into – and be (friendly and supportive yet) robust in your challenges. Life it too short to be wasted working on no-hope proposals.

The fifth qualification question - Jon

I have a confession to make. Long, long ago, when I was running the proposal centre for a major IT organisation, we set about improving the business's qualification process.

Soon, sales staff were used to the mantra – is it real, do we want it, can we win it, can we do it? They started to expect us to probe, debate, play devil's advocate, facilitate objective decision-making.

This particular proposal centre found itself in the fortunate position of being able – to an extent – to pick and choose which deals we supported. Before very long, one of the salespeople I'd known in my days as a purchaser arrived at our door. To say I didn't rate the individual would be an understatement, but we humoured him and supported his well-qualified opportunity. As was his wont, he then contrived to turn the golden egg into a recipe for disaster and threw away what should have been a sure-fire win.

We conspired. What could we do? Soon, I struck on the solution with my senior team. Sure, the business's new qualification process had four questions, but our bid centre's list extended to a fifth: is it real, do we want it, can we win it, can we do it, and is the account manager's name Fred Smith? Needless to say, we were after 'yes' answers to the first four questions – and one 'no' to the last.

Soon, Fred was on the phone. "I've got an RFP coming in next week: can you help?"

"Next week, Fred? So sorry, but we're booked solid for at least the next month."

"Right. Worth asking, though. Anyway, I've got another one coming in in three months' time."

"That'll be October, right?"

"Yes. They're due to issue it on the 12th."

"The 12th? Oh no. Not the 12th? I mean, we're clear at the very start of the month, and we've got loads of capacity towards the end. But the fortnight around the 12th is our one busy period that month. Lots of holidays, three other big bids already scheduled. What bad luck."

"Ah. Oh well, at least I'm in time to let you know about the proposal we'll need to submit in December. That's sixth months away."

"And I'm so grateful to you for letting me know, Fred. It's always great to get such clear advance notice: we really appreciate it. But we're not able to forecast more than three months out: could you call me again in October?"

When to stop - Jon

We often talk about the need to justify the decision to bid – using our proven mantra: "Is it real? do we want it? can we win it? can we do it?"

Sometimes, though, it can be just as powerful to focus on the negatives. Here, then, are my top six warning signs that you should 'no bid':

1 You're not the incumbent, and can't clearly identify areas of real dissatisfaction and pain for the client with their current provider, and/or can't deliver the solution at significantly lower cost due to some inherent efficiencies in your approach. (This is likely to simply be a benchmarking exercise, with no real possibility that they'll change).

2 Your salesperson hasn't met the customer face-to-face in the last six months. (People, after all, buy from people they know, like and trust – and, given that the buyers will inevitably have been speaking to someone to gauge the market, that must therefore have been your competition).

3 You've been given an unrealistically short time in which to respond to a detailed RFP. (They know who they want to choose, but now have to be seen to go through a process).

4 The specification in the RFP uses your competitor's language and terminology. (They know who they want to go with - and it's not you!)

5 You don't have the people around to produce a high-quality proposal in the time available. (You're unlikely to dislodge a competitor if you don't clearly come top when the proposals are scored. And the lack of a stampede of people wanting to help in itself says something about your chances of glory).

6 It's not in your sweet spot – you'd struggle to deliver the solution successfully, and lack clear, relevant references of delivering similar solutions for other clients. ("Trust us; we'll work something out" is unlikely to give them the confidence to jump ship).

If any one of these is true on your current bid: stop. Now!

Pin these up on the wall next to your desk. And next time you're asked by a salesperson to chase some mythical pot of gold at the end of an apparent rainbow, feel free to use them in anger.

The flag of surrender - Jon

An amusing debate the other evening discussed props that we use when running proposals. The usual range of items came out – post-it notes, pre-printed flipcharts, laminated cards with questions that provoke debate, toys in the war rooms to reduce stress and engender creativity. I recalled BJ's black plastic rat, brought out so that anyone in a session could wave it prominently should they feel that the discussion was disappearing down a rat hole!

And then I remembered my white pocket handkerchief, from my days running a corporate proposal centre. A team in a qualification meeting I was observing was poised to decide to 'no bid' a major deal, without adequate, objective debate. Rather, they seemed too bruised by recent losses to want to return to the battlefield – despite the fact that the opportunity was eminently winnable and deliverable.

Yours truly duly reached into his pocket and pulled out the clean, white handkerchief. Slowly and solemnly, I started to wave it in the air.

"OK, Jon, go on…." (The sales director was used to my maverick ways by now!)

"It's a flag of surrender."

"Pardon?"

I went on to explain that it seemed to me that if the team were to turn away from this opportunity, they might as well all resign and go and work for the competition. Soon, the debate was focusing on what the team could do to win the opportunity if they really put their minds to it; confidence started to creep back in to the debate; they were on their way.

Now, it's not the role of proposal managers to own the qualification decision. But we do act as coaches, as motivators, and we should never lose sight of the importance of this element of our value add.

With a stressful week ahead… - Jon

I rolled up pretty early to a client site the other Monday morning, to set up for the day's training course.

Their sales director – one of the very best in the business – was listening to, and occasionally participating in, a 'bid / no bid' conference call. The hoped-for outcome was the latter course of action, and he was merrily helping the participants talk themselves into that not-always-easy decision.

What struck me as interesting was the timing of the call, not something to which I've ever given much thought previously. But if you want to get a team to qualify out of an opportunity, which time would you choose:

- 8am Monday morning ("you could have a straightforward week, or it could be stupidly busy and stressed if you take on all this extra work")

- some time on, say, Thursday morning – when the participants are already deep in hero-worker mode ("look at how much I've done this week!") and not yet that fussed about or focused on the following week's schedule.

On: proposal strategy

The storyteller - Jon

"So, what do you do for a living?"

That was the question posed to me by a cab driver the other day, as we waited for a friend who'd popped into a laptop repair shop to come back out and join us in the car. And, to be honest, it's quite a tough one to answer, if the person answering isn't used to the world of business, sales, procurement. "Proposal manager? What's one of them, then?"

My son Benedict used to ask me a similar question when he was much younger: "What do you do at work, daddy?" I guess if one's an engine driver, a police officer, a teacher, it's easy to respond. But how to explain to a small child about the world of proposals?

My answer, which seemed to satisfy him? "I go to work to help business people to tell stories."

Now he's somewhat older, and he knows much more of what I do, I think he's a bit disappointed that my working life's not quite as glamorous as 'storytelling' might imply to a child. But I actually think it's a pretty good summary of what we do.

Same solution, different customer, different story - Jon

There's a new-ish Spanish restaurant in town, which we decided to try for the first time the other day.

The staff were really friendly: mainly students at the local University trying to avoid sinking ever-deeper into debt. Our server handed us the menus, and explained the choices, describing the wonderful selection of tapas but noting that: "Unfortunately, the paella takes about 45 minutes to prepare. The chef has to prepare it fresh each time."

'Unfortunately'.

So guess what we had? Yes, that's right. With our love of fine food, why would we possibly go for the quick-to-serve dishes that they'd grab, pre-prepared, out of the storage jar, when there was a cooked-to-order option for much the same price?

And as it was prepared fresh, we were even able to swap out the squid, which I hate, for some extra chorizo.

An interesting indication, this, of the importance of tailoring your story to the specific customer. No doubt plenty of their customers are after rapid refreshment en route to the pub; for them, "steer clear of the paella" would be exactly the right message.

Yet for us, on a Saturday lunchtime with a large pile of newspapers to browse, in no particular hurry to go anywhere? Why, the 45-minute wait for the chef's special was just the thing.

Re-gift - BJ

I'm guessing many of you will be familiar with the term 're-gift'. The term is used when a gift that has been received previously is then given to someone else and presented as a new gift.

I wasn't familiar with this term until this past holiday season, during which I'm fairly certain I received a couple of 're-gifts'. I received gifts which had obviously not been chosen with my taste in mind and/or had obviously been given to someone else. One even appeared to have been rewrapped in the same paper, which was quite crumbled and ripped when I received it. (Since I know you'll ask, one was a 'TacoMan Tortilla Maker' and the other was a 'Hot Cocoa Set'.)

When I received these so-called gifts, I felt like I didn't really matter to the people who gave them to me. I viewed their giving them to me as purely perfunctory and I felt that they had put no energy into thinking about what I liked or what I'd hope to receive.

To me, they had expended the absolute minimum amount of energy necessary. The effect of receiving these gifts was such that I would have felt better had these people said, "Sorry, I didn't get you anything."

I can't help but think a customer receiving a proposal that presents no value or benefits, is non-customer specific and largely cut and paste feels the same way.

Knowing your audience - Jon

We often swap anecdotes with colleagues in Strategic Proposals, and one such note recently provided the perfect illustration of the importance of understanding the customer's evaluation team before you start to write a proposal.

One of his previous organisations submitted an investment proposal to a major UK retailer. The document and subsequent bid presentation were packed full of advanced technical information that could only be fully understood by evaluators with detailed knowledge of the investment and pensions market.

Unfortunately for them, the potential client, being a relatively enlightened organisation, had invited trade union representatives to act as two of their four pension fund trustees. The bid team were unaware of this, and their slick suits contrasted somewhat with the overalls worn by the two truck drivers on the opposite side of the table.

Half way through the presentation, one of the union reps interrupted:

"Bob and I tried to read your proposal but didn't understand a word of it. We haven't understood a word of your presentation either... We honestly don't know the difference between an equity and a bond. And we don't really want to know.

I've promised that I'll take the wife for a cruise when I retire in ten years' time. If we invest our pension money with you instead of the other people who've presented, will I be taking her round the Caribbean – or will we be catching the ferry to France?"

Client-centric messaging - BJ

I was in a local store which had a fair number of things that were breakable and/or potentially dangerous for children. Many a store I've been in has had a sign along the lines of "Please watch your children" or "Parents are responsible for any damage done by their children".

This particular store had obviously given some thought to the individuals to whom the sign was directed (the parents), as well as to some potential motivators that would cause the parents to heed the sign. It read:

"Unattended children will be given an espresso and a free puppy."

The several children I saw in the store were being held firmly by the hand and closely watched by the parents.

Are the messages within the proposals you submit as compelling to your clients as this sign?

Three for the price of one - Jon

Working with a client on a proposal the other day, we played with the age-old proposal strategy mantra: "Why us, why not them?"

Their draft document was relatively strong on the 'why us' angle – with clear customer insights, strong proof points (case studies, quotes, research findings), a coherent and well-explained solution. But still somehow the story, and the proposal as a whole, felt lacking.

So we broke the statement down into its components – making sure the team understood that there are actually three questions in one, each of which needs to be covered:

- Why? – the proposal has to demonstrate that there is (and that the bidder understands) a strong rationale to deliver the initiative

- Why us? – giving confidence that the bidder can deliver an excellent solution

- Why not them? – the ways in which the bidder's approach differs from, and is more desirable than, the offers that will be received from their competitors.

Brainstorming each of the three topics in turn – rather than, as usual, treating it as one question – drove out some fascinating insights. I'd urge you to try the technique in your next strategy workshop.

What we know - Jon

My current favourite way of challenging the salesperson owning an opportunity?

"What do we know about the client and opportunity that none of our competitors will know?"

Try it sometime: it's amazing what it can unlock – either excellent insights that help with your proposal strategy, or a conclusion that you're really not as close to the client as you should be (and as others actually are), and so potentially might want to qualify out of the bid!

I'll tell you what I want... - Jon

It's [2006] ten years to the day since The Spice Girls hit the top of the music charts in the UK with their debut single 'Wannabe'. Its chorus? "I'll tell you what I want, what I really, really want."

If your document is going to prove truly compelling for the customer, you need to get under the skin of the buyers' real needs. As those of you who've heard us speak at conferences will probably recall, we're therefore great believers in what we term 'The Spice Girls' Theory of Proposal Strategy':

"Tell me what they want, what they really, really want."

A great proposal doesn't just answer the very logical questions in the RFP: it has to hit the right notes for the buyers at an emotional level.

Sent out of the room - Jon

Discussing strategy development with a team recently, I found that two course participants had both peer-reviewed the same proposal for their company, a couple of days before the event. An easy demonstration of powerful strategies came to mind.

I asked one of the pair to leave the room for a few moments, and asked the other to use the flipchart to list the key messages that he could remember from the proposal. We covered it up, then brought his colleague back in and asked the same question.

Not surprisingly, their output varied somewhat – each having come up with differing lists of half-a-dozen or more themes.

It wasn't a huge leap to imagine the evaluation team having been left with similarly muddled messages as to the reasons why they should have selected this supplier. And as an illustration of the need for a proposal to focus clearly on three or four key messages, and to present these in a memorable way, the exercise couldn't have been more powerful.

Like father, like son? - Jon

Some readers may be familiar with one of my pet phrases, a 'Benedict Proposal'. Benedict's my son. At the age of two, his first ever words were, "Me, me, me, me, me." And the majority of proposals I see work on similar lines – they're far more supplier-centric than customer-focused.

After all, it's much easier for a bid team to discuss their own organisation and its capabilities ("Me, me, me") than it is for them to write about the customer!

The young gentleman in question is now [2007] seven – or, as he would phrase it, 'almost eight'. He's just demonstrated that his proposal skills are improving with age. His school is running an appeal to raise funds for a major extension to their buildings; to publicise this, they recently ran a competition in which each of the pupils had to submit a picture of a room that should be incorporated into the new block.

Benedict picked up one of the three prizes. His design? Well, the competition was being judged by the teachers. So a picture of a beautifully designed, comfortable, superbly equipped staff common room was always going to win, wasn't it? Particularly when the other kids were all drawing state-of-the-art, Wii-filled play areas!

Talk about producing a submission that hits all of the evaluators' hot buttons spot on, and differentiates your efforts from the competition! (And no, since you wonder, I didn't have anything to do with it!).

Bidding to Voldemort - Jon

Comedian Jo Brand told a wonderful story of how she handles audiences, at an event to which we took a group of Strategic Proposals guests last night in London.

It helps, she said, to think of the audience as a person. To paraphrase her examples: the late crowd in the comedy club might be a drunk man. A gentler group in a more upmarket venue could be a diner in a vegetarian restaurant. And one can then adapt and adjust one's style on stage to strike the right note and have the right conversation.

I immediately made the connection to our world, and I think I'll try this out in proposal strategy workshops moving forward. "Were the client a person, who would they be?"

I've done bids to evaluation teams who seem to be aloof, superior and 'know it all'. I've done others to teams who seem to be in panic mode, desperate for help. Some can seem distant, slightly uncertain of themselves. Some come across as confident yet engaging.

Perhaps just the characteristics would be enough. Perhaps we could come up with a caricature (verbal, or sketched). Or we could even try to come up with specific names: "This bid's going to Winston Churchill". "The client here's James Bond". "This lot are Voldemort".

Politicians, actors, comedians, literary figures, movie characters, musicians, sportspeople – the imagination could run riot. I'm curious to see how it'll work out. If you try it yourself, let me know. And if you can put a face to the name for any of your recent proposals, do tell!

"I always say 'Message matters most'. It doesn't matter how many leaflets you put out or doors you knock on, if you don't have a relevant message for the voters, then you won't win." - Lynton Crosby, election strategy guru

"What keeps me awake at night is the thought that the person I'm competing against will have thought of something I haven't." – Sir Clive Woodward, former England rugby coach, APMP UK conference, 2013

On: price and value

My Grandma's Coffee Cakes - BJ

My Grandma makes the world's most critically acclaimed coffee cakes. And if you care to argue the point, you'll have to take it up with the company. The company being 'My Grandma's of New England Coffee Cakes'.

I recently purchased one of these wonderful cakes and I highly recommend them. But be forewarned: they're a bit expensive. Part of the cost is in the vanilla they use – "100% pure real bourbon vanilla ($92.00 per gallon)" – as they explain in the literature provided with each cake.

They go on to state, "We'd rather explain the price than apologize for quality." I think that is a very powerful statement and certainly goes along ways in the "it's all about price" argument.

Cheap – but decidedly not cheerful - Jon

I was party to an interesting debate recently amongst a group of proposal managers from different companies, who discussed techniques for winning with a higher price than their competitors.

Most of their debate centred on the philosophy that BJ uses to great effect when training salespeople about proposal strategy: "If you don't create value, all the customer has left to go on is price". So they talked about creating empathy with the customer, working out win themes, drawing out points of differentiation from competitors and suchlike.

Perhaps they were just being polite, but – observing from the sidelines – it struck me that they missed playing on the fear factor that lurks for so many evaluators.

Two of the more powerful messages to weave subtly into your proposal if you're worried about being the more expensive bidder are:

- "You want the cheap solution?" (which may be below the minimum acceptable quality, creating problems for your users and business, causing you considerable headaches on an on-going basis – and casting doubt on your competence: "bring me the heads of the fools who selected this incompetent supplier!")

- "They think they can deliver it for that?" (because if they do, their cost model must be wrong – and their solution flawed – or they're misleading you: you'll be forever fighting against change requests and price increases as they exploit their 'price to win, recover to profit' strategy).

If it's all about price… - BJ

…then help me understand Starbucks.

It's all about price if… - Jon

Your proposal strategy is all about price if you can convince the buyer that:

- you have the most efficient solution to meet their requirements, consuming the fewest resources

- those resources are cheaper than anyone else's

- your stakeholders require a lower return on their investment – i.e. margin – than your competitors'.

- the fact that you'll give them the lowest price will be embedded contractually, underpinned by benchmarking (for what that's worth)

- none of your competitors will outsmart you in the way they present their price (e.g. 'bid low, recover to margin', 'buy the business') or will underspecify their solution

- no competitor can offer a significantly higher return on investment – i.e. quantifiably larger benefits for their higher price

- cheap really is cheerful for the customer's team – not fraught with risk and hassle

- the customer trusts you.

If you're not confident of all the above, then your story really can't be all about price, can it? You have to create value – and a good strategy process becomes essential.

But it's all about price, right? - Jon

I'd arranged to grab a coffee yesterday with a good friend who's very senior in the world of procurement. As usual when it starts to pour with rain, I'd forgotten my umbrella, so I was sheltering inside a Waterstone's bookstore across the street from his office. (Hey, any excuse to browse, right?).

He came and dragged me out. As we left, he commented on a prominent display of paperback novels priced at 99p each. "They must be dreadful books if they're selling them that cheap," he commented.

Actually, they're all from acclaimed authors – some even shortlisted for the prestigious Booker Prize.

Market Price - BJ

I was just out in Seattle, delivering an APMP Foundation Level Accreditation workshop and presenting at the first Fall Symposium held by the Pacific-Northwest Chapter of APMP.

As one does when visiting in Seattle, I went to the Pike Place Market. The market has at least half dozen stalls selling fresh fish. One stall in particular, the Pike Place Fish Market, was quite busy, and much busier than the other stalls.

I was aware of the Pike Place Fish Market, and I suspect some of you are as well. This company is famous for the way they work. They stop people walking by. They engage potential customers in conversation. They are loud. They shout out orders. And, most intriguingly of all, when a fish is ordered it is thrown to, and usually caught by, the person packing it up. The people working here have so much fun, are so much fun to watch, and are so engaged with their customers that a video of them is part of a management training course that is used by other companies.

I visited all the stalls in the market and from what I could tell the prices from one stall to the next were, for the most part, comparable. But that's where the comparisons ended.

The Pike Place Fish Market stood out from all the other stalls. When I approached the person there, he smiled, told me his name, asked me what my name was and where I was from. He then asked me which of the fish I'd like to sample. He let me try several, while at the same time explaining how the fish was caught, prepared, etc. He was very knowledgeable, and I asked lots of questions. He seemed genuinely happy to answer them all.

This person kept me engaged in a pleasant conversation and there was never any pressure to buy anything or for me to rush. He seemed to truly enjoy conversing with me (I know Jon, hard to believe, right?). He also seemed to very much enjoy his work.

While he and I were speaking, orders were being taken, shouted to the back and fish were flying. The atmosphere was infectious, and people gathered to watch, many of them engaging with the staff, trying samples, etc. I bought quite a bit of fish to take home with me.

Now, I suppose I could have, maybe even should have, checked prices at the other stalls. But I didn't. Instead, I bought my fish from this person who had taken the time to establish a 'mini' relationship with me. We'd hung out together, even if only for a few minutes. But those minutes were fun and memorable. By the time I had decided which fish I wanted to purchase, this person felt more like a friend than just a sales person. I would have felt disloyal going to another stall, even if I did save a bit of money.

The Pike Place Fish Market certainly debunks the myth of it being "All about price".

"So what?", twice - Jon

An interesting discussion recently on the age-old topic of 'features versus benefits'. Sometimes I find that one has to ask, "so what?" twice (or more) to get to the real benefits.

Here's one example I rather liked:

"Our laptop has fingerprint security."

"So what?"

"Well, that improves security, as users don't have to remember their password. And there'd be fewer calls to the help desk, too."

But, to me, that only took it so far. "So what" again revealed some much stronger benefits:

- Less time spent by Help Desk solving password issues (= saving in IT support costs)

- Less time wasted by end-users requesting and awaiting password resets (= cost saving too)

- Lower risk of fraudulent or unauthorised access to your information (presumably there'd be data to quantify that as well).

It's a fun game – and good mindset to be in when working on proposals.

Size matters - BJ

I have been considering getting a new lawn tractor and was recently speaking with a sales person for one of the popular brands. (I won't mention which, but the sales person's name was John and he was such a dear).

I had done a bit of research and had determined that, given the size of the lawn I mow (close to two acres) and the tasks for which I use the mower, this company's smaller offering (call it #1) was too small and that I needed either their mid-sized lawn tractor (call it #3) or larger still (#5).

When I told him the size of the lawn and the various tasks for which I would be using this piece of equipment, the sales person said I need to consider a larger machine, such as #7.

I stated, "Certainly, either #3 or #5 will do the job." The sales person confirmed that I was correct. "Either of those two machines will do the job and do it well. The problem is you'll wear out the machine much faster."

He went on to explain, "#3 or #5 will take much longer to mow your lawn, probably as much as twice as long. And because it's taking longer, you'll run the machine faster than you should in order to get done sooner. Running the machine faster will result in pushing it too hard and this will in turn cause it to break down sooner. You'll also not do as good a job mowing because the mower is moving faster than the proper pace to get a good cut."

As happens so often, there's an obvious parallel here with many of the proposal groups on which we conduct benchmarking and assessments. Such groups are all too often understaffed. This is further exacerbated by those individuals being expected to perform all of the various proposal functions, and often also be the pseudo subject matter expert.

The above scenario results in the staff working harder and faster and this in turn results in poor quality proposals, staff burn out and people eventually quitting. Such groups would do much better to staff appropriately and realize the long-term gains… in both improved proposal quality and associated win rates, as well as overall cost savings.

I'm going with the #7. It will cost me a bit more at the start, but the benefits – machine life, quality and overall costs – more than offset this.

On: structure and writing

Something's missing – BJ

While picking up my coffee this morning at my local Dunkin' Donuts, I noticed a sign on the counter. The sign, promoting their omelet on a bagel, read:

The ingredients in your omelet are –

- red bell peppers

- onions

- potatoes

- mushrooms

- bacon.

As I read this I had a nagging feeling that something was missing here. After a few seconds, it hit me.

Did you notice it? Right. Seems that whomever put this marketing piece together (and it was nicely done and had a very official looking #54328-91B on it, so I'm guessing it came from corporate) was so focused on all the extras, they missed the main ingredient.

Need I point out the parallel to some proposals? :-)

The bookcase theory of content design - Jon

"Why bother with all of this storyboarding?" an account manager asked me recently. "I much prefer just to get on with things."

Have you ever bought a set of shelves as a kit from a home furnishings store, ready for self-assembly, I wondered in return? You certainly can build something if you unpack boxes and start bolting stuff together. With good luck, it might even resemble the pristine bookcase you so admired in the store.

Sure, it may look a little unsteady on its feet; there may be a few parts left over ("I never quite worked out where that piece was supposed to fit"). You may need to de-construct some sections once you realise that you've used the wrong materials. It'll take you much longer overall. And I certainly wouldn't recommend that once you've finished, you line up your most precious and fragile ornaments on the shelf below your heaviest books.

That's why they include a set of plans showing how everything should fit together. The same approach applies to proposals. You can just start typing. But it's really worth mapping out a high-level answer to each RFP question first.

Just don't take the analogy too far – there's an art to developing good storyboards that make the team's life easier, whereas some furniture shop construction plans seem to be designed for use by those with doctorates in engineering. Make your process and documentation too complicated, cumbersome or confusing and your content contributions may just ignore your good work and make things up from scratch anyway!

I Can Name That Tune in Three Notes - BJ

Those of you who are old enough might remember the title as the tag line for the show, 'Name That Tune'. On the show, the objective was to recognize a song having heard the least number of notes. (Yes, Jon, this probably was before your time though I am starting to think you might not be quite as young as you'd like to think you are!)

I think our job as proposal professionals has an element of the above to it. That is, we need to be able to present information using fewer, rather than more words. Sometimes this is stated (RFP instructions – "The Executive Summary may not exceed 1500 words") and sometimes it is just following 'best practice' (Proposal reviewer – "Uh, I think this 35,895-word section on our company history might need to be edited down a bit").

As proposal professionals, I think we should keep this concept in mind – and seek to use fewer, rather than more, words.

The shorter the better - Jon

I present to groups of purchasers on a fairly regular basis.

I've taken to asking for a show of hands: "Tell me if you've evaluated proposals in the past six months for a particular purchasing project."

Ninety per cent of hands go up.

"Keep your hands up if the longest proposal won the deal."

Like a flash: not a hand left in the air.

Introductions - BJ

I recently listened again to the song 'The Walk of Life' by Dire Straits. This song has, in my opinion, a wonderful intro – and as I listened to it, I started thinking about intros within proposals – both as part of an Executive Summary, to individual sections and within responses to specific questions.

The intro to this song, like any great musical intro, does several things: it introduces the key signature (E Major), the chord progression (in this case E A B A B E if I have it right) and the chorus. And it repeats all of these several times.

In this case, the intro truly made me eager to hear more (this might have been influenced by my knowing the song!*)

Overall, the intro gives the listener a taste of what is to come and makes them want to hear more.

And isn't this what the introduction to an Executive Summary should do? Set the tone, give a flavor of how the information will be presented and make the reader want to continue reading?

Give a 'listen' to the intro to your Executive Summary and see if it 'catches your ear'.

--

*I think familiarity plays are a big part in proposals as well. Clients who know you well and to whom you've previously presented proposals will have an expectation as to what they will 'hear' from you.

Exec Summaries – the buyer's view - Jon

Our dear friend Sheilagh Douglas-Hamilton is one of those rare folks whose career has straddled senior roles in both purchasing and proposals, with great success. She's been back in the world of procurement for the past few years, but we still end up debating proposal issues together on a regular basis.

One recent discussion concerned the role of the Executive Summary. Sheilagh fired the following across to me the next day by email, and was happy for me to share it with our readers:

"The purpose of an Exec Summary? To blow me away so I can say, 'Yes! Yes! Yes! They really do understand my business and what I want!'"

A good Exec Summary "shows that not only do you understand my requirements, but why you are the one to deliver them." It should provide "a clear, concise summary telling me at a glance, in easy to understand language, why your offering is the best."

And here are Sheilagh's views on the characteristics of a successful Executive Summary:

- is beautifully written

- uses nice language (with no mistakes, please!)

- is clear, concise and compelling

- tells a story

- is short and punchy

- makes no more than three pitches

- makes me want to read the rest of the document to find out more

- doesn't contradict the main body of the text!

I always find this sort of input from an experienced evaluator's perspective really useful. How does the Exec Summary of your most recent proposal fare against her criteria?

Appendix-itis - Jon

How about this for a remarkable piece of writing, from a proposal we reviewed recently:

"Detailed biographical details are included in CV's in Appendix C and in Tables 3a, 3b, 4a, 4b, 4b, and 5 and in Appendix G."

Like, as an evaluator I'm going to bother – rather than just rolling my eyes heavenwards and sighing deeply...? You could be forgiven for imagining that the amount of paper-turning that would be required would turn the proposal into some clever origami model.

Our esteemed colleague Richard Jenkins described one recent proposal as suffering from 'Appendix-itis'. Sure, there are times when material needs to be moved to an Appendix – most often if its length would disrupt the flow of your story.

But this should be the exception, rather than the rule – a last resort to be carefully justified each time. And, at the very least, the main answer should include a synopsis of the material that the evaluators would find were they to read the Appendix – ensuring that you get the maximum score whilst recognising that reviewers probably won't read the detail on their first pass through.

They would say that... - Jon

On a trip to Kuala Lumpur, I browsed the dining recommendations. Werner's was proudly described as "The best Italian restaurant in Malaysia", no less.

Impressed? I was, until I noted the footnote in small print – 'as voted by the owner's mother-in-law'! Now, the humour made me smile, but it's an interesting illustration of the power of a proof point: something so important in proposals.

Awards won, benchmarking data, comments from clients, quotes from the press or from analyst reports – they all help to bring your story to life. And our research suggests that evidence and references that substantiate your claims are highly prized by evaluators. Albeit, of course, it's not unknown for companies drawing on analyst reports in their proposals to have commissioned the very research they're quoting in the first place!

Accentuate the Positive - BJ

More and more often these days the response I receive when I say, "Thank you" to someone is, "No problem."

What I'm left with here is "problem".

I much prefer and will continue to use the positive version and reply with, "My pleasure" to a "Thank you" from someone.

The shoe-shopping theory of proposal proof points - Jon

A wander through one of London's nicer areas after dinner with a friend recently [December 2013] took us past the window of a shoe shop. There, it proudly proclaimed its award-winning track record as "Women's Footwear Retailer of the Year: 1999, 2000, 2004, 2005":

"So what does that tell you about them?" I asked, interested to test a theory.

"That they've been really useless for the past couple of years," my friend immediately replied.

There's always a fine line when mentioning prestigious awards in a proposal. The fact that you were acclaimed 'Company of the Year' this year means you're at the top of your game, the very best in the industry. Why wouldn't the buyers buy from you?

If it was the last calendar year's prize then, hey, they might not yet have got round to holding the awards ceremony this year! But two or more years ago? There's someone better than you out there who has been walking off with the silverware.

Even if you're not the remaining champions, there can certainly be value in quoting a long list of successes that demonstrate a consistent level of excellence year-in, year-out. But if said list stumbles to an abrupt end three years ago, it feels to the potential customer as if you might be a little tired as a supplier, and that they might be better shopping elsewhere.

Safe content - BJ

A respected colleague and fellow proposal professional sent me the following piece of content. This is for a response by a company that provides transportation. (The name of the company has been changed to protect the incompetent.)

"Terrific Transport believes each day begins and ends with compliance. Your members' safety is our number one priority and we will make the safety culture part of the call center and our relationship with each transportation provider. We will not compromise on safety and we will guarantee that safety will be the number one priority of Terrific Transport in the operation of the contract. Terrific Transport is committed to leading the way to world class safety. Through the dedicated efforts of every team member and programs designed to lead subcontracted transportation providers, Terrific Transport has become known as the safest and most reliable passenger transportation service in the world. Terrific Transport has many safety programs that are geared to making safety a visible and daily part of all of our operations. The Terrific Transport safety program is discussed at length in Section 7 of the proposal response."

As you can see, it is stated numerous times within this piece of content that safety is important to Terrific Transport. Too bad there isn't a single piece of evidence that demonstrates that the customers' members will be transported safely and/or that safety is important to Terrific Transport.

The Lucy theory - Jon

The guy opposite me on a train home from Manchester one recent evening was chatting away loudly on his phone to his young daughter, Lucy.

He told her that he'd been giving a presentation; she clearly didn't understand what that meant, and so he explained:

"A presentation is when you tell a story to lots of people about all the work that you've been doing recently."

Funny, isn't it? Our proposals and pitches spend so much time telling the client what we will do in the future, once appointed, that we sometimes miss the trick of telling that what we have been doing.

And yet, where clients so want to know that you have created a solution specifically to meet their needs, it can be incredibly powerful to explain something of the process you've been through to assess their requirements and design your offer.

Loved and hated = losing - Jon

Proposal teams always talk about the need to appeal to the interests of all members of the evaluation team. And, of course, said team is likely to be multi-disciplinary in nature – comprising representatives of each of the business functions with an interest in the decision and the solution.

There was an interesting illustration of this principle in a discussion recently with a senior purchasing manager. He talked about a recent evaluation, where three bidders were in contention for a particular contract. Bidder A came out clearly on top of the scoring with half of the evaluators; the other half of the team were passionately in favour of Bidder B. Needless to say, Bidder A's fans hated Bidder B, and vice versa.

The result? Bidder C won – fully capable of delivering the solution, liked by all of the evaluators (but loved by none) – and second in everyone's scoring... Of course, you'd really want to come top of the table with everyone – but it's the illustration of the importance of appealing to all of the evaluators that struck me as a particularly pertinent lesson.

In Other Words - BJ

The latest edition of the Merriam-Webster dictionary has about 100 new words/phrases.

One of the words/phrases on the list definitely relates to proposals. The word/phrase is 'gray literature', which is defined as 'hard to get written-material'. I think most of us can relate to this.

Missing quotes? A trick of the trade - Jon

"But we can't get any client quotes!"

Most proposal teams understand the value of using customer quotes in their proposals to substantiate their claims and add credibility to their story. You know the sort of thing:

"Our requirements were identical to yours. This supplier – or should I say, 'partner' – have done truly fantastic things for us. They delivered early, exceeded all expectations, and charged a pittance. Our users are delighted. Our customers are ecstatic. Our revenues have shot up, and our costs declined drastically. We trust them completely. They're a joy to work with. I've personally been promoted, twice, since they did the work for me. I would recommend them wholeheartedly: I think they walk on water. Please feel free to call me at any time of day; I'd be delighted to chat to you."

But what if you're writing a proposal and you simply can't get a customer quote – or (perhaps as powerful in some circumstances) a comment singing your praises from a market analyst, benchmarking report or press article?

One simple tactic – not ideal, but better than nothing – can be to use internal quotes. Consider the relative impact of each of the following:

- We are committed to ensuring that our project managers are trained to the highest standards.

- "We are committed to ensuring that our project managers are trained to the highest standards" - Jon Williams, Senior Vice President, Programme Management Office

Neither's a perfect piece of proposal prose – but the personalisation of the latter gives it a certain extra credibility and impact.

Unintentional negatives (accentuate the positive) - BJ

Jon and I have written and spoken many times about 'unintentional negatives', wherein the focus is actually on something negative rather than positive as intended.

I came face-to-face, quite literally, with the first example while attempting to relax and unwind in the bath a few days ago. As I lay in the tub I found myself staring at the bottle of bubble bath sitting on the edge, which proclaimed in large letters: "STRESS AND TENSION RELIEF".

So, there I was, trying to relax, staring at a label that emphasized the things I was in the bath to get away from: "Stress" and "Tension" (the word "relief" was lost on me by these two words.)

On the back of the bottle the company used words like "soothing", "calming" and "relaxing". I wouldn't have minded seeing those words while soaking in the tub and those are the words that should have been on the label. After all, that was my focus while using the product – and it's the focus of the person purchasing it.

Writing: secrets of success - Jon

A common query came up again on a recent course for the proposal team of an asset management company: "So how do we make sure our proposal content is first-class?"

This would be my wish list:

- A house style guide for proposals, written in an entertaining and accessible way, giving all contributors pointers on how to develop good content

- Training for all contributors. I said "all". Not just the proposal team. Training serves two purposes – it helps people to improve their content, and also takes away some of the 'fear factor' they face when working on proposals.

- Great pre-written proposal content. Write it once, to the highest standards; keep it up to date; make sure everyone who needs it has access to the material, using a professional tool

- Clear briefing of all contributors. Make sure they have appropriate detail on the context for this proposal, the themes you're trying to put across, the messages you'd like them to cover in this particular answer, the expected length of the answer you'd like back. (Ideally, make sure that – if they're contributing lots of content – they're involved in the strategy and storyboarding sessions!). And give them plenty of time and advance notice!

- Professional editing by the proposal centre. You'll never ensure absolute consistency of voice throughout the document if you're collating information written by individuals with different writing styles and abilities. That's where great proposal writers come in.

The wine bottle - Jon

I spent a rather lovely day out grape-picking recently – a birthday present last December from my friend Carrie that had to wait to be enjoyed until the autumnal harvest was ready. I say 'picking' – we did a little of that, but it's perhaps fair to say that the subsequent tour of the winery (yes, we do make wine in England!) and tasting consumed the larger portion of the time we spent at the vineyard.

Later, we went for dinner with her partner, and decided that more wine was called for – and on the list, I spied this rather complex explanation:

"After a huge investment of both time and money this wine is now presented with a stelvin closure to preserve freshness and purity of fruit, whilst also avoiding the possibility of cork taint."

Anyone guess what 'stelvin closure' means?

Yep, you got it: 'Screw cap'.

It sounds like the sort of thing I read in proposals all too often – content contributors feeling the need to write over-elaborate text, incorporating jargon wherever possible, as if doing so makes them sound clever. And, of course, it usually achieves the exact opposite. Never forget to keep it simple!

Eloquence - Jon

I've been toying with statements that encapsulate the value that a proposal writer can bring to the subject matter experts who contribute proposal content.

One I particularly liked – probably to be used with senior managers, rather than with the contributors themselves (who might feel just a tad patronised!) is:

"To make them sound more eloquent than they actually are."

On reflection, however, this may be aiming too high. Perhaps we should stick with:

"To remove the need for them to be eloquent at all."

The Demise of the Concept Album - BJ

While I was selecting songs from my iTunes library recently, it occurred to me that the way I listen to music today is very different than it was 'back in the day'. (And yes, I can hear Jon now, "Do tell us BJ: What was it like back when music consisted of strolling minstrels?").

I'm talking about in the 70s or 80s when music was done as an album, and the artist intended the songs to be listened to in a particular order. One song introduced and led to another and the album as a whole told a story.

In today's world of downloading single songs and creating playlists in whatever order the listener chooses, music is listened to in a very different fashion and the idea of listening in a particular order is certainly well out of the control of the artist.

Listeners today pick and choose which songs they like, sampling here and there, selecting the songs they like, leaving others behind. They put songs in the order they feel works best for them. Based on my experiences reviewing and evaluating proposals, there is a corollary to this in the world of proposals.

A reviewer might read a proposal from the beginning and work through it in the order in which it is presented. But it's just as likely that, certainly as a first pass, they will scan the document, choosing to read some sections, stopping where something catches their attention and skip others, especially if it appears on first glance that it will be laborious to get through.

So it's our job to make sure that each individual section captures and holds the reviewers' interest and reads well as a standalone section. We can't expect or count on a reviewer having read the sections in order and we can't assume they'll have the requisite information from one section before reading another.

When developing proposals, we need to make them work as both a single piece as well as having each section stand on its own. We need to capture the reader's attention at specific points and be prepared for reviewers to 'pick and choose' information to meet their needs. This requires planning, time and specific skills. And it sure does make our job challenging, doesn't it?

Tailoring your proof points - Jon

A charming email popped up in my inbox the other day from a total stranger:

"I'd like to add you to my network on LinkedIn as I feel that we may be able to offer some support to yourselves. We currently work with a wide range of different companies including providing IT purchasing support for [top property company] and onsite support for [major bank]."

I've taken out the names of the clients concerned, but otherwise reproduced it verbatim.

Interesting, isn't it, how the use of inappropriate client references can undermine your story, rather than enhance it.

As an evaluator, I want the confidence that follows from knowing you've done similar things for other clients in the recent past; that your work is viewed as successful by key individuals in their organisation and that you have delivered real, quantifiable benefits. "Are you confident they can do it?" is an important challenge that I need to be able to answer, for my own peace of mind and to reassure any senior executives on high who have final sign-off on the contract award.

But, as a principal director of a business with 25 or so staff worldwide, "we've done work with major corporations" hits all the wrong notes for me. "We don't understand the needs – or the financial cost base – of companies like yours" is an entirely counter-productive message, and a salutary lesson in how not to use proof points.

Writing Music - BJ

When you're writing, do you prefer to have it quiet or do you listen to music?

When I'm writing I prefer to have music play. As I write this I'm listening to some old Tom Petty and the Heartbreakers' as I ride the train into New York City.

I actually have playlists on my iTunes that I've put together just for writing. My choice of music varies from heavy metal (Iron Maiden) and rock (AC/DC) to bluegrass (Alison Krauss), folk (Cheryl Wheeler) and everything in between (reggae, classical, soul, etc.) And I can see my pal Jon cringing as he reads this list.

I know others who find it difficult, if not impossible, to write if music is playing. I think Jon falls into this category (though interestingly, after all our years of working together, and sharing lots of music with each other, I don't know for sure.)

So, do you listen to music while you write? And if you do, what kinds of music do you prefer while writing?

Cutting down - Jon

Providing peer review support for a client over the past couple of weeks. On day one, I checked with the account manager: "Is there any limit on the length of our answers? It doesn't specify one in the ITT…"

"This came up in the bidders' conference. There is. It's 2,000 words." A good day of critiquing rough-cut first drafts followed, and we kicked the material back to the contributors with encouraging comments as to how they could sharpen their answers.

Fast forward to the start of the following week, when I rolled up on site to work on the next drafts of their material. But something was nagging me about the responses: such an important limit being mentioned in the bidder Q&A but not elsewhere? Despite the robust assurances I'd been given: odd.

I made the account manager call the client, just to double check. He turned ashen-faced.

"It's not 2,000 words. It's 2,000 characters."

Fortunately, we were still nearly two weeks away from submission, with decent drafts in hand or due within a day for each of the 33 answers. An intense burst of decimating their answers – many of which at this stage were over even the

2,000-word target – duly followed over the next 36 hours, cutting them down to much nearer the acceptable size. And then it was back to the subject matter experts to review the newly scythed drafts, check them for accuracy, and spend the final week of the bid polishing up the content still further.

"Excuse me writing you a long letter: I didn't have time to write you a short one." Indeed…

Troubling language - BJ

Like many of our readers and fans of the written word, I love the subtly of our language. I came across a great example of how a minor shift in words can make a significant difference to the message.

In a recent newspaper article a company involved in an accident wherein a customer was seriously injured stated, "We have established a policy that we do not comment whenever we are under investigation or involved in litigation."

Upon hearing this, I couldn't help but think of the message this sends. If you are like me, the message this sends to you is that this company is under investigation/involved in litigation so often, they have had to establish a policy to ensure employees don't provide comments in such cases.

Had this company worded this differently they could have delivered the message they probably intended. They might have stated it something like, "As we are currently involved in litigation, it would be inappropriate to comment." Said this way, the message is, "We behave appropriately when we're litigated" and "We're involved in litigation at the moment", rather than often or continuously.

Of course, making sure the message being sent is the one the writer intended takes time and careful consideration of the words used and their order. That's why an appropriate amount of time needs to be allowed for rewriting and editing content when developing a proposal. It's also why proposals which are rushed out the door often unintentionally deliver the wrong message.

Asking a monkey - Jon

A friend who's a schoolteacher commented to me the other evening, about one of her more challenging teenage pupils:

"He's incredibly articulate, but when I ask him to write anything it's like asking a monkey to colour in a picture."

I challenge you not to conjure up that image next time you're working with a salesperson who's brilliant in meetings and when presenting, but who struggles to convert that into similarly eloquent proposal prose!

Part of our role, as proposal professionals, is to take away the fear factor that so many of our business colleagues experience when it comes to the written word – allowing them to focus on the customer and proposition, drawing on our help to articulate their great stuff as powerfully and persuasively as possible.

Sesquipedalian - Jon

A few years ago, BJ taught me a new word: 'sesquipedalian' – defined as:

"Characterized by long words; long-winded."

His contention? That the adjective applies to far too much proposal content. We want writing to appear natural, conversational: if you couldn't imagine reading your answer aloud to the evaluators across a table in a meeting room, it's probably too formal.

Yet content contributors seem to feel the need to use grandiose words and phrases, as if this will impress the readers. (After all, at school you got higher marks for using more advanced language to impress the teacher with the range of your vocabulary, right? The same just isn't true of proposals. You're writing to win a contract, not the Nobel Prize for Literature.)

Three recent examples of unnecessarily complicated writing have caught my eye of late, the first from a proposal which noted that:

"The project will be delivered within a three-month timeframe."

That's like asking "how long do you need for lunch today" and finding your group saying: "We'd like a 45-minute timeframe, please." They wouldn't: they'd ask for "45 minutes" – just as: "The project will be delivered within three months."

The second comes from the coffee machine outside a meeting room in which I've been working regularly. Aside from the cappuccinos, lattes and americanos, it offers "hot water". The sign next to the machine usefully adds the explanation: "A portion-controlled hot water selection". Just in case you were in any doubt...

And the third? Also drink-related, from a recent stay in Vegas. Here's the blurb from the packaging:

"Good things in Small Packages. The Revolution is our award-winning single serving box with one infuser inside."

A teabag, if you were wondering. (Actually, "a unique tea gift", to be strictly accurate).

Quality not quantity - Jon

My favourite comment from a proposal evaluator recently, reported to me by a salesperson:

"For whose comfort are all these pages?"

Just a perfect reminder of the need to write concise content!

Confusing the reader - Jon

Spotted recently, pinned to a hand-dryer:

"This facility is unavailable due to essential maintenance works."

... because 'broken' really would have been too simple.

Along similar lines, on a trip to Versailles a month or so ago:

"The tour continues on the opposite side of the peristyle."

OK, make me feel stupid. Peristyle? Where do I go now? Oh – you mean the walkway with columns that I'm standing in.

Why is it that people writing notices – or proposals – feel the need to try and impress the reader with overly grandiose language? And don't they realise that, in their attempts to impress, they actually achieve the very opposite?

Do you write? - Jon

There are so many skills associated with developing a first-class proposal: project management, team leadership, facilitation of each stage of the proposal process, design, document management and many more.

But what of writing? The longer I work on proposals, the more I come to appreciate that lots of the best people at managing proposals out there are actually pretty mediocre wordsmiths.

So: you work in the world of proposals. What are you like as a writer? Honestly?

My test, I guess, is whether you write for pleasure. I find that most folks who can write proposal content that really flows invariably also write outside office hours – perhaps a blog, or fiction, or for some society or local journal.

Writers write – incessantly, addictively. And if you don't – if your skills are in some of the other, equally critical elements of the proposal process – perhaps you need to surround yourself with a few wordsmiths if you want to inject a little magic into your proposals.

Speed Bumps - BJ

Reading my morning newspaper today I came across three different things that I refer to as 'speed bumps'. Though perhaps minor to some people, these not only caught my eye but literally derailed my reading.

The first was coming across the word 'funnest', as in: "This was the funnest thing I had ever done." If I had read this in the "Letters to the editor" I might have been able to let it pass. However, I came upon this 'not a word' within a column that is nationally syndicated (actually internationally, as I've read it when I've been in Europe) and read by millions.

This bothered me enough to cause me to check an online dictionary to see if perhaps this had become an accepted word. I did find 'funest' (pronounced Fyoo-nest), meaning boding or causing evil or death; fatal; disastrous but this certainly wasn't what the writer intended as they wrote.

In that same paper, I read a piece in the "Goings on about Town" about a spate of burglaries in a nearby town. I then read the exact same article under "Our Neighbors". (I read about 1/3 of the article before I realized I had already read it. I then went back and checked to see if I was just tired and hadn't had enough coffee or if in fact this article had been duplicated.)

My morning reading was less than enjoyable at that point. And then I came across a picture with what was obviously the wrong caption. I did get a good chuckle out of this as the picture was of a family at a picnic and the caption read, "Town meeting results in clash of ideas."

Will this make me cancel my subscription? Probably not. Has it changed my opinion/impression of the paper and the people that publish it? Yes, it has.

I've no doubt that 'speed bumps' have a similar impact on the people reviewing/evaluating proposals.

Forget lunch, I'm going to bed - Jon

Waiting for a friend recently in a rather nice fish restaurant in Edinburgh, as a gentleman and lady arrive at the next table.

He's obviously been here before, because he immediately comments, in a matter of fact way, "I'm just going to have a lunchtime quickie."

"WHAT?" she shrieked in sheer surprise.

He looked puzzled – then blushed, and passed her the menu. "Lunchtime quickie: £7.50, Monday to Friday. Mussels or seafood chowder with crusty bread, chips and a glass of wine."

I suppose we do that in proposals, too – assume that the reader's familiar with a particular phrase or concept. But I doubt it has quite as shocking an effect!

Follow The Bouncing Ball – If You Can - BJ

I recently came across a small piece in the New Yorker, excerpted from the Wall Street Journal, that demonstrates how easy it is for something in writing to have various meanings and often for the unintended meaning to be very humorous, and quite distracting.

In this article, Andrew Concors, a physical therapist and certified industrial ergonomist at San Diego-based CPT consulting, is speaking about the use of a 'gym ball' instead of a chair. No doubt you've come across someone in an office sitting on one of these things. The gym ball, also known as a Swiss ball, is said to better for your posture, physical well-being, etc., than sitting on a chair.

Andrew points out that the gym balls are not without risk, stating he is aware of several patients who have ruptured their balls while sitting on them. Ouch!

Did they really write that? - Jon

Thanks to one of our friends, who runs the proposal team for a major financial institution, for emailing us an extract from a recent proposal, which she thought might entertain readers here. Names changed to protect the guilty!

"Practically we would see this working as XYZ initially offering all of your ABC business to us as cases come up for renewal and you seek new opportunities, however we know that in today's dynamic and competitive market place we may not always be able to meet your's and your client's needs so we believe the preferred partner status gives you the flexibility to work with us but also to benchmark other providers either on specific cases or specific classes of business where the client's demands and needs cannot be satisfied by our programme."

Yes, folks, that's 94 words. As I always say, if you read the sentence aloud and run out of breath, it's way too long!

May I be of Service? - BJ

I recently spoke with a call center representative for an airline. English was obviously a second language for this person, though he spoke English reasonably well.

He helped me make the needed change to my flights and we exchanged pleasantries. His closing comment let me know he had been trained to express that it had been a pleasure to be of service to me when concluding the call.

However, something was definitely lost in translation, as what he said was, "I have had a great time servicing you."

I had all I could do not to reply, "It was good for me too, guy."

Second Languages - BJ

I was on a tour bus in New York City recently while hosting a relative from Turkey, Ilayda, who's visiting for the summer.

The people on the bus, as one would expect on a tour bus in New York City, were from other countries and didn't speak English as their first language, if they spoke it at all. Ilayda, for instance, is just learning English, has a vocabulary of a couple of hundred words and can make herself understood, but is only just learning the language.

I was therefore somewhat surprised by the wording the tour guide used when he explained the need for people to be quiet. He could have simply said, "Please be quiet." Or he could have stated this very simply with, "No noise please."

Probably the most effective way to convey what he wanted would have been to put a finger to his lips and said, "Shhhhhh."

Instead, the tour guide said,

"If you must converse while we're meandering through the city, please keep your conversations as brief as possible and to a minimal roar."

Now I ask you, even for those who have a basic understand of English, what do you suppose the chances are that they'd be able to understand this person's request?

No doubt you'll already be making the connection to proposal content. The job of a proposal is not to impress the reviewers/evaluators with our fancy vocabulary and language abilities. It's to state the information clearly and in a way that is easy to understand. As you've heard us say many, many times, "Keep it simple."

Only a 'hint', mind... - Jon

Overheard in an office recently... a desperate account manager wandering from desk to desk, looking for someone who could help with content for a proposal due the following day:

"I need someone who can make it up, with just a hint of techie."

I was rather encouraged that, even in his moment of crisis, he was still sharp enough to want content that was written in a style that would appeal to the relevant evaluators.

Adventurous - BJ

I saw a sign advertising a dry cleaner recently. The company promoted their services as being "For the adventurous".

Huh? Adventurous? I'm not sure I want to be adventurous with my clothes.

For a vacation? Sure. Bring it on. My last vacation was to Costa Rica and I was looking for adventure. But for my good suit? I don't think my suit needs any excitement, thank you very much.

This is clearly a case of the 'theme' not matching the client's needs. (There can't be market for people who wish to be adventurous with their dry cleaning, can there?)

Unfortunately, it's not uncommon to see such a mismatch when a company's overall theme is applied to a specific client who has different needs than those promoted by the overall theme. Thus the need for customizing/tailoring of theme statements.

New Term - BJ

During a recent discussion with a proposal team, one member struggled quite a bit before he was able to articulate a question he wanted to ask. He just couldn't find the right words.

The question was whether a particular aspect of our offer could or would be evaluated and if so, what kind of weighting it might receive from the evaluators. I realized we needed a new term for just such a situation and offered for the team's consideration and future use, 'evaluweightable':

"Evaluweightable. Adj. "Is our being able to implement the solution in significantly less time than requested within the RFP evaluweightable?"

Feel free to use this when and where appropriate.

Have a favorite new term of your own? Please let us know. Perhaps we'll start a glossary.

Less is quite enough – Jon

Here's the review of a restaurant called 'Brussels Sprouts', from the Luxe guide to Singapore.

"The malty brews and steaming hot moules are must haves at this breezy bistro and bar. 01-12 The Pier, Robertson."

Excluding the address, that's 16 words. The other guidebook I was using for reviews when I was there last year featured a description of the same restaurant that ran to 532 words, and said little more that would have helped me to decide whether or not to eat there.

Then there was the 22-word review of a trendy-looking fish place I wandered past:

"Dress down and prepare to get messy. No Signboard Seafood is over-bright, noisy, bustly and famous for its white-pepper crab."

Again, I can pretty much get the gist of what the place is going to be like, and whether and when I might want to go. Now, I'm a fairly experienced traveller, and pretty used to finding places to eat in far-flung cities. Had I been a novice to overseas travel, or a less regular diner, I might have appreciated the extra detail. So writing to meet the needs of the reader is clearly key.

But I did think that this was a cool illustration of the power of succinct, sharp writing. And I'd hazard a guess that the writers at Luxe spent far longer polishing their twenty-or-so words than their competitors did over their five hundred plus.

"The limits of my language define the limits of my world." - BJ

A proposal writer with whom I was working recently (howdy there Mikey) was wearing a t-shirt bearing the title of this post. The t-shirt also had a photo of the person to whom this quote is attributed, Ludwig Wittgenstein (Austrian philosopher, 1889 – 1951)

I've no doubt this quote resonates with many (or perhaps most) proposal professionals.

Certainly the limits of our capabilities with the written word directly affect our ability to create a high-impact, high-quality document. And I'd suggest we're also similarly limited by our ability to create graphics.*

So what are you doing to expand your language abilities? Like any skill, over time our abilities using language diminish if we're not doing what is needed to keep them as sharp. I know a great many of you are, like Jon and I, avid readers and I'm sure this greatly contributes to language skills (assuming you're not just reading trash! :) I know quite a few proposal people who attend writing classes and/or workshops, and lots of us keep a journal and write on a daily basis for the sheer joy of writing and to keep our skills up.

A side note – I did a bit of research on Mr. Wittgenstein and, based upon two of the other quotes attributed to him, I suspect he might have done some time as a proposal professional himself. He is said to have stated, "I don't know why we are here, but I'm pretty sure that it is not in order to enjoy ourselves." That sounds to me like something someone might say late at night in a proposal center.

He is also said to have opined, "If people never did silly things, nothing intelligent would ever get done." And we all know it's the 'silly things' that lead to 'magic' on proposals, right?

--

*If a picture is, as the saying goes, 'worth a thousand words', it stands to reason that for each graphic we don't use, we add another thousand words to our response.

It's All Relative - BJ

I caught a commercial on the radio today introducing a new doctor at the local hospital. The commercial closed with the doctor stating, "I treat all my patients like you'd treat a member of your family."

Okay. I understand the intent here...but I think you can easily see where this could be confusing or out of alignment with the listener's thinking. (Oh sure, like I'm the only one with a few dysfunctional family members, right?)

As we all know and have heard many, many times, it's all about understanding the client.

What did they just say? - Jon

My all-time favourite worst-line-ever in a proposal (ignoring those involving proofreading errors) was in an Executive Summary that I reviewed in my purchasing days, which stated:

"This is described in more detail in our quality assurance procedures, which may or may not be included later in this proposal."

As an example of breaching the rule that a good proposal should 'read with one voice' – in terms of both the style and substance of the content – this must take some beating.

The Shape of Things - BJ

The author of a recent Associated Press article likens the shape of the island the article references to that of a "spark plug".

Now, I happen to know what shape a spark plug is (as I've changed a few in my day) but I'm pretty sure Jon wouldn't!

As I read this I couldn't help but wonder what percentage of the people reading that article would know what a spark plug is shaped like (without doing a quick search on the web!)

I think this is something we need to consider when we use comparisons or analogies in our responses. To work, the basis of comparison used has to be something to which we're confident the majority of the readers/reviewers can easily relate.

Words - BJ

Dewar's scotch is running an ad on TV that presents the following quote (which they attribute to one Tommy Dewar):

"The less a person has to say, the more words they'll use to say it."

It seems to me this is often the case with content within proposals, and especially within executive summaries. I certainly see my share (and I'd guess many of those of you reading this will have as well) of executive summaries that are long, rambling and without any apparent key message or even the remotest of plots.

It's as if the person creating these documents thinks if the content is long enough they'll eventually stumble onto some sort of message. Or perhaps they're just trying to lull the reviewers to sleep (and I've no doubt their submissions succeed in doing that!).

I do see crisp, concise exec sums that have a clear message and tell a compelling story (and I hope many of you have as well). My experience is that these are created by individuals who have a solid grasp of the customer's concerns/issues, have a clearly defined position for their offering and know why they are submitting a response. They know what they want to say, and they say it... in as few words as possible, rather than the other way around.

The historical perspective - Jon

Apparently, the word 'proposal' was first used in the English language "before 1550".

That sets my mind spinning in creative – and silly – directions. One can imagine, for example, Michelangelo working late into the night in 1546. His task? Responding to Pope Paul III's Request for Proposal for the design contract for St. Peter's Basilica in the Vatican.

I wonder whether they had pizza delivery in Rome in those days, to help when they were trying to pull their proposals together at the last minute, by candlelight? At least the client would be confident that the quality of the graphics in his proposal would be pretty high...

Any Storm in Port - BJ

A good friend of ours sent us this response to an RFP question (and I could hear her infectious laughter as I read it!).

The RFP question:

"If your administration office(s) were to be destroyed in a hurricane, where would you relocate, what functions would be resumed in 24 hours, 72 hours, and 1 week?"

The response:

"(Company name, withheld to protect the embarrassed) would only be mildly inconvenienced if a tornado were to hit the building."

Don't Go There - BJ

While reviewing content within a knowledge base for a client, an associate who shall remain nameless (big shout out to Diane!) came across the following and sent it my way. I'm posting it here for all of us to enjoy together. From an answer regarding disaster recovery:

"Data is backed up and stored in a geographically adverse area."

Perhaps this is to suggest the bad guys in that particular part of town will keep others away?

Mangled in translation - Jon

A hotel I used recently in Germany was undergoing refurbishment prior to the influx of visitors for this summer's soccer World Cup, which starts tonight.

The staff couldn't be more friendly and welcoming and are doing a truly fantastic job in the circumstances. (Said circumstances including the ever-present potential for a friendly builder's face to appear outside your window from the scaffolding surrounding the building – whilst their colleagues dig out a new car park under the hotel).

What caught my eye, though, was an apologetic line on my booking confirmation letter, which warned of this construction work:

"We would request provident and courtliest for your appreciation for optical and temporarily acoustical interferences."

That's worthy of many proposals: contributors often feel under pressure to write the next Pulitzer prize-winner, and use overly complex language when it would be so much more powerful were they to express themselves simply.

Whenever I see a thesaurus on the desk in front of someone working on proposal text, I'm tempted to throw it away (or, at least, charge them a pound per look, to make them think carefully about whether they need their writing to be any more flowery). Not, of course, that there isn't room for beautiful writing in proposals; it's just that your writing needs to be appropriate to the context.

It also sparked thoughts about multi-national proposals, where some contributors are writing in languages other than their mother tongue – or where text is being handled by a professional translator. These situations need real care: not least, to make sure that these contributors don't feel patronised or insulted when you edit their text. (That's true, of course, even with contributors working in their native language, many of whom also struggle to express their thoughts in writing correctly and coherently).

Now my own foreign language abilities are pretty limited, and I have huge admiration for anyone who can hold forth in more than one tongue. So I'm not being in any way critical of the often-fantastic efforts that come from multi-national teams. But I do think a few recent favourite lines scribbled on my travels might be in order:

- "It is very important so-called process owners participate actively during project implementation." (Proposal from Eastern Europe). OK, so we know they don't really *own* the processes...

- "In the event of any problems, the concerned project manager would review the situation". An interesting difference in word order between Indian English and English: glad to hear that said project manager would be so upset!

- My favourite: a notice outside a proposal team's office in Belgium, publicising the activities of the company's "Health & Safety Prevention Committee". I adore the idea of a committee sitting down to work out how to prevent Health & Safety.

Any other favourite examples gratefully received!

Winning within word counts - Jon

"... and then you find that your draft answer's 700 words long, and have to decide which of your points to leave out."

So said a salesperson on one of my recent courses. And, sadly, I do fear that that's the reality on most proposals. Do you go into less detail about your solution, chopping out useful material? Spend less time showing you understand the client's needs, creating less empathy? Include fewer proof points or make less attempt to bring your win themes to life?

There is, of course, a better way. A professional proposal writer will edit content to say more with less.

I discussed this recently with the four specialist writers working in SP's UK team. Their view? The word count on the beautifully polished versions they produce is typically between 25% to 30% lower than that of the drafts they receive from subject matter experts.

What's more, the text reads far more fluently and persuasively.

Say more within your word count, and say it better. Some sales organisations fail to see the value of proposal writers: to me, they're totally missing the point. Perhaps this blog entry will help!

Trying too hard? - Jon

I've been lucky enough to have spent the past nine days working in Budapest. For those who don't know Hungary's capital, it really is one of Europe's loveliest cities.

Work-wise, the trip was a roaring success. Feedback scores on the six courses I ran – for over 110 attendees in total – was, in order, 98%, 99%, 93%, 94%, 98% and 95%. The delegates' comments were generous, too. Whilst 'happy sheets' at the end of the day don't always correlate with real business impact, I left with confidence that we'd engineered a step change in motivation, confidence and capability for the participants. Near-shored proposal teams can bring such benefits to their organisations. They can also face such challenges. Helping the mainly young, invariably enthusiastic course participants to navigate some of those was a delight.

Alongside the lovely people were the delights of the city - especially, here, some excellent food and even better wine. Under the tutelage of my favourite UK wine merchant, I've come to appreciate the joys not only of a good Tokaji dessert wine, but also some of Hungary's finest reds, rarely exported. Top-notch Cabernet Franc from the Villany region, for example, or the sensational yet scarce Barbar.

I ate this time in two outstanding restaurants - at my cost, I might add, not the client's! The first holds a Michelin star, yet is the most relaxed and informal place you could imagine. Sitting outside. Wearing jeans. Joking with the waiters.

And eating food that was simple yet sublime. The second, not yet starred - although recommended by Michelin. An excellent meal. Yet trying just a tad too hard.

Outside tables... crisp tablecloths.

Relaxed informality... staff taking themselves oh-so-seriously.

A short yet excellent wine list... a tome.

Plain tableware... appetisers arriving on beds of polished stone, amidst forest twigs.

Food that seemed almost surprisingly marvellous... dishes that just tried too hard to impress. ("Please use the pestle and mortar to crush the herbs we have cut freshly for you, in their bed of liquid nitrogen, before we add your wild apple sorbet"...)

A meal that had won that coveted star... and one that felt so desperate to do so.

And if my week working with the proposal folks highlighted one thing, it was the need to create that apparently effortless rapport with the client. To write proposals that create genuine empathy, showing passion for delivering the proposed project professionally. That takes real effort. Real skill.

But, you know, I can't help thinking that some proposals come across like the second restaurant: as if they're trying too hard to impress. The true art is in creating documents that feel naturally engaging. How do yours fare?

Writing with style - Jon

I was fascinated to read a review yesterday in The Times of the new [2017] edition of their Style Guide.

This – along with The Economist's equivalent – used to be one of my standard reference manuals when writing proposals. Yet language changes so quickly that, these days, I'd rather use an online version. Any printed document's going out of date by the time it's published, and in a few years its advice may not prove to be contemporary. The Guardian's online version is especially good for

British English, I find. Where the arrival of a new Times edition is interesting is therefore less as a go-to guide for daily usage than in the changes since the previous version – which Amazon reminds me that I bought on 7th April 2013, shortly after it was published.

It picks up, for example, on how capitalising words has fallen out of fashion. When I started evaluating and writing proposals, it was common for "the Project Manager to hold a Quarterly Steering Group Meeting at Head Office". Now, in the UK at least, we don't do that!

It's part of the overall trend towards more conversational content in proposals. Twenty years ago, many read like glorified dissertations or dull project reports. Now, if you can't imagine reading your answer aloud to the client – and it seeming natural, engaging, friendly, professional and appropriate to the audience – it's probably too formal. As BJ has always said, your proposal is a packaged sales presentation – just not one you're in the room in person to talk through.

That's not a call for informal language, mind. One of the worst drafts I've reviewed in recent months had swung too far in the opposite direction, coming across as colloquial, overly informal and patronising. If it reads like a Facebook status update, it's probably too casual. There's a balance to be struck, as in most things.

And as proposal specialists, more attuned to writing styles than our sales or technical colleagues, it falls to us to continually champion good practice. A great proposal should be a joy to read. When did you last train your proposal specialists to be better writers? And when did you last coach your contributors to write content that's persuasive and contemporary?

On: layout and design

The wrong road - Jon

A team I know well recently showed me the front cover of a proposal they'd submitted for a construction project upgrading a major road. The image? A beautiful photograph of a highway, heading into the distance at sunset.

"Very neat to have used a photograph of the road," I commented.

There was an embarrassed silence, before the eventual confession: "It's not actually the road... It's just a stock image."

We always talk about using appropriate images on the front cover. A photo of the road on which they'd be working would be great. One of a different road entirely creates precisely the wrong impression.

(And why stop at a photo of the road as it is now? A debate on the choice of images might include an artist's impression of the road after its upgrade; a map of the route – especially if there was any clever differentiation, such as finding a shorter path for it to save money; a combination of before and after?)

May I Have Your Attention Please - BJ

Researchers have discovered that we have two distinct types of 'attention' (and actually use different parts of our brains to process each). One type is the one we use when we are focused and anticipating what is coming next. The other is when something comes along unexpectedly and our focus is drawn to it.

To have the greatest impact, the proposals we develop have to address both types of 'attention' of the reader/reviewer. We need to maintain the interest of those who are highly focused as they read/review our response and we have to capture the attention of those who are skimming it or flipping the pages.

This is why we so strongly emphasize the need for considering both the 'information' (what the response says) and the 'presentation' (how the information is presented) aspects in the development of strategic proposals.

A restaurant analogy - Jon

A little over a year ago, I moved home, from one end of the country to the other. A day or two after we'd arrived, a leaflet popped through the door advertising a new Indian restaurant, opening that evening about five minutes' walk from our new house. Not having unpacked our cooking utensils by this stage – and having already tired of takeaway pizza – we decided to try it out.

The place was lovely. Nothing too upmarket – but with comfortable decor, friendly staff and truly excellent food. We loved it – and went back. Repeatedly. Indeed, before long we felt something of a moral obligation to return to offer them our support, so often was it the case that we were the only people dining!

Not surprisingly, something had to change if the business was to stay afloat. In came new waiters, new paintings on the wall – but, thank goodness, the chef and the food stayed unchanged. And still the residents of our town stayed away in droves.

Finally, shortly before Christmas, the owners gave in to the inevitable, and closed their doors... only to re-open them again, a month or so later, having completely redesigned the place. A sophisticated new name, trendy furniture, the coolest crockery, a leather-bound menu that had clearly been designed and produced at huge expense. And... wait for it... exactly the same chef and exactly the same food. Yet the prices had increased drastically – by 25% or more.

Guess what happened? After a year of nigh-on solo dining, we now find that we can hardly get a table, so busy has the place become. They're queuing out of the door; reservations are required; the owners have already doubled their capacity by refurbishing the upstairs floor.

And what's this got to do with proposals? Well, the restaurant's always had a great product at its heart – the food. That's not changed. It's just the way that they've presented the story that's improved, to suddenly hit the 'sweet spot' of so many local residents. And revenues and margins have increased dramatically.

Spot the similarity? No matter how good your company's products or services, if you don't package them up in a way that appeals to your customers, you're destined to fail – and when you get it right, the buyers will flock to choose you.

A glass act - BJ

I've often said to Jon, an expert on wines, that I believed any effect using a certain shape wine glass for a particular wine had on the taste of the wine was all in the drinker's head. My belief was confirmed in the book Predictably Irrational (Dan Ariely, Harper).

The book states, "If you're really serious about your wine, you may want to go all out and purchase the glasses that are specific to burgundies, chardonnays, champagnes, etc. Each type of glass is supposed to provide the appropriate environment, which should bring out the best in these wines (even though controlled studies find that the shape of the glass makes no difference at all in an objective blind taste test, that doesn't stop people from perceiving a significant difference when they are handed the "correct glass").

Moreover, if you forget the shape of the glass really has no effect on the taste of the wine, you yourself may be able to better enjoy the wine you consume in the appropriately shaped fancy glass."

I think this is similar to the effects of good proposal packaging. That is, though points are not typically awarded for appearance and packaging, when reviewing a proposal which is professional in appearance and packaged in a way that makes it easy to handle and review, the reviewer will be inclined to be less critical of the content and award a higher score.

I wonder if we could get Mr. Ariely to conduct a controlled study to prove this (though I'd guess it wouldn't work too well having the reviewers blindfolded!).

Who needs captions? - Jon

I've often mentioned one of my proposal bugbears – overly lengthy captions for proposal graphics, which distract from the flow of the document. I'm on something of an anti-caption campaign altogether at the moment, having reflected at length on the advice in the APMP Foundation exam that a great caption should "invite the reader to draw the correct conclusion from the graphic".

See, if your graphic is good enough, you shouldn't need a caption to help the reader to draw the correct conclusion: that conclusion should be evident and obvious from the graphic itself.

I'm not arguing (altogether) that you should dispense with captions entirely: sometimes they can be useful, and sometimes they can be expected by the evaluators. But I would argue strongly that captions are often simply making up for the inadequacies of the graphics that they support. Next time you need a caption to explain what you were trying to illustrate, maybe it's time to re-draw the graphic itself and make it clearer, and more focused on the customer and on the benefits of your approach?

Proposals: your shop window - Jon

I'm fresh from an interesting debate with a company which has a heavy high-street presence selling to consumers. Their shops are wonderful: state-of-the-art retail design, trendy, eye-catching, impressive. They're now doing more and more work in the business-to-business space.

In the B2B market, their proposals are their shop window. Yet the documents are thrown together by one long-suffering member of the sales support team ("and we really struggle when he goes on vacation....").

In a same vein, I often like to pick up copies of the latest marketing leaflet in the reception area of the companies I visit. Glossy, professional photography, copy-written to the highest standards – yet I doubt a brochure ever won a single piece of business. Meanwhile written proposals, which do have a huge impact on customers' contract awards, suffer from continuing under-investment and neglect.

And while I'm talking about B2B proposals, I'm reminded of my theory that proposals are never really 'B2B' documents. They're 'P2P' – about the people in the bidder's team writing documents for the people sitting around the buyer's evaluation table!

Working Outside the Box - BJ

Several Strategic Proposals team members are currently working with me on a proposal effort. This effort was underway when we were brought in and had been in the works for some six months or so prior to our becoming involved. Despite having been worked on for a seemingly long time, not much progress had been made and much of the content had not been developed.

As we reviewed status on the project, we discovered what was slowing things down. We learned that the people who were responsible for the content – the subject matter experts (SMEs) – had been given a format to use and asked to submit their content in that format. The format consisted of various boxes on a page, each a specific size and designated for a particular type of content.

As many of these SMEs had little to no understanding of how to work within the formatting, each time they worked within a box, either the content didn't fit, or it would corrupt the format. As a result, they would spend as much, if not more time, attempting to correct the formatting as they did working on the actual content. They also often limited the amount of content they provided in order to make it fit within the specified box.

Recognizing that the formatting was what was slowing down the SMEs, we immediately issued instructions to have them work without the format. They were instructed to focus solely on the content. We asked them to identify which box the particular piece of content would ultimately go in, and we did let them know they should be as concise as possible, but we told them not to concern themselves with formatting. We let them know formatting would be handled towards the end of the effort and that it would be done by someone who was an expert at formatting. They collectively gave a sigh of relief.

This simple change had a huge impact. The SMEs, no longer having to deal with formatting and able to focus solely on content, produced better content and did so much quicker.

Are you perhaps making the task of content development more difficult than it needs to be by attempting to work within a format, rather than making the formatting of your document a discrete step at a later stage in the process? If so, you might want to consider 'working outside the box' on your next effort.

The challenge of proposal and pitch design - Jon

I spend so many nights in hotels around the world for work that I'm pretty careful in my choices of where to stay. That makes the odd disaster - such as the place I was in in Budapest earlier this week [2017] - somewhat surprising, and rather frustrating.

Someone had clearly put a lot of careful thought into my room's design. The brown decor. The plastic chairs (inspiring, no doubt, the phrase "Designer chair concept" on my reservation confirmation). The cut-out, numbered footprints on the wall. (Yes, really).

The problem was that that careful thought had clearly been around a decade ago - so it all felt incredibly dated, and slightly shabby. My suspicions were confirmed when I looked at the list of prestigious awards the place had won - from the likes of Conde Nast. In 2008.

It reminded me of a comment I scribbled on a proposal that a client in London asked me to review recently: "This looks very 2012."

"Fabulous," they said, falling into my trap, remembering that most wonderful of British summers. "The Olympics. Gold medals."

"No. Just a bit dated."

See, proposal design's moved on faster than almost any area of our profession.

In the States, Mike Parkinson's seminal book ('Billion Dollar Business Graphics') was key to pushing people towards higher-impact, more client- & benefits-centric design. On our side of the pond, SP organised and sponsored the first award for proposal design in 2008, in association with APMP UK - trying to trigger the profession here to think differently.

Then, for a few years, the Strategic Proposals UK team produced an annual 'black book' - a nicely bound portfolio of the best work by our designers. These days, it's in a PowerPoint deck: updating it in hard copy once a year would seem too infrequent, such is the pace of change in the level of proposal design needed to keep ahead of the pack. Indeed, I happened to glance the other day at some of my team's 2014 work - which gained wonderful plaudits at the time and helped clients capture many big deals - and grimaced at how dated it now looks.

As I commented in an APMP conference presentation a few years back: people see what it looks like before they read what it says. And if your documents today look like they did even three years ago, they simply won't look contemporary.

Of course, people argue, more and more proposals have to be submitted via online portals which restrict design creativity. There's not much you can do if it's Arial, 10 point, no illustrations. In fact, all that's meant is an explosion of creativity at the presentation stage (or, when it comes to 'orals', as many in the profession in the US rather, erm, surprisingly call the pitch phase). Those buyers who are incredibly over-prescriptive when it comes to RFP responses offer us virtually free rein when we go in to present.

These days, a great proposal not only needs to "superbly articulate a compelling story" - to quote BJ's memorable phrase. It needs to be brought to life superbly visually, too. And if you don't have the resource and skill in your team to achieve that, you'll almost inevitably be falling behind your competition.

"Page design is about striking a compromise between beauty and clarity."
- Kari Pedersen, Art Director (News), The Guardian

On: creating creativity

The book review - Jon

Early on when running a proposal, I ask members of the team to visualise success. If they all have a clear and consistent picture in mind of "what good would look like", then the chances of them "doing good stuff" will be that much higher. The process should be less painful, too, as they work with a common goal to which they've each committed.

One team I worked with recently was struggling to get their minds in gear on this topic. We'd tried the usual tricks: we'd brainstormed, we'd used post-its, we'd visualised the evaluators reading the document, we'd drawn pictures – but to no avail: nothing really clicked.

So I tried an alternative approach the following morning. I copied the back covers of a selection of paperback books – novels and non-fiction. I asked the team to look through them and study their composition. A headline to catch the eye, a plot synopsis, an author profile and a few gushing quotes seemed to be the common features.

And then I invited the team to write their own perfect back cover for the proposal they were about to write. And it worked like a dream!

Yet I was minded to push the concept a step further. Most evaluation teams will produce some form of internal briefing note about each bidder's proposal. That summary, it struck me, is broadly akin to a book review.

So, what if we asked proposal contributors to write a 'review' of the 'book' they're about to produce – specifically, the review they'd hope would be written by the customer's chief evaluator? That'd make them think about structure, style and story of the proposal they were about to develop – and might well unlock some great ideas.

The power of a three-letter word - BJ

All too often we reply with: "But…" – a term I describe as "a verbal eraser" as it doesn't honor what the other person has said.

In order to communicate effectively, I suggest replying with, "Yes, and…"

In this way, the other person's idea is allowed to stand, rather than being erased, and that individual will feel that their idea has been heard and considered.

The Anti-Problem and other cool tools - Jon

Whilst the candidates sat their APMP Foundation exam yesterday during a course I was running in our Utrecht office, I raided the bookshelves of my Dutch colleagues.

One very cool volume was 'Gamestorming', by Gray, Brown & Macanufo. I particularly liked their concept of 'The Anti-Problem': ask the team to solve the problem that is the *exact opposite* to the challenge that they're currently facing. I can see lots of applications:

- Describe the *worst* possible solution and supplier

- If we wanted to persuade the client *not* to choose us, what would we say in the proposal?

- To develop proposals in our organisation in the *least* efficient and effective way, what would we do?

I also loved 'Brainwriting'. Identify the topic you want to solve ("Improving our proposal capabilities", perhaps). Give each participant a large blank card on which to write an idea relating to the matter at hand.

Get them to pass the card to the person on their right – and ask each individual to add an idea to the card that they have just received, to enhance or build on what they have just read.

Keep on circulating and adding to the cards. (If you use paper instead, the authors suggest passing the sheets on by turning them into paper aeroplanes...!)

A couple more: conduct a 'Pre-Mortem' – rather than "what are the risks?", ask "how did this end in disaster?" and work backwards.

Or hold a 'show and tell' session in which at the start of the campaign you ask your contributors to bring and discuss one thing that could contribute to your success on the bid (for example, something that they have delivered for another client with similar needs).

Let us know if you play with any of the ideas! I certainly intend to...

On: leading

Out of the Mouths of Babes - BJ

A friend of a friend related the following incident recently (via his Facebook page).

"While in horrendous traffic today, constantly being cut off left and right, moving at a snail's pace and generally getting myself all riled up, my 3 year old turned to me and said 'Daddy, you need to calm down. Let's take a few deep breaths together. Then we can find a playground, you can swing for a while, and we'll all feel much better.'"

I've been on many proposal teams that could use someone with this kind of wisdom.

It's not about '-ed', it's about '-ing' - BJ

There's a reason we refer to proposals as 'live engagements'. It's because the development of a proposal isn't a static, one-time event. As we all know quite well, it's a complex series of many activities, many happening in parallel and many dependent on the preceding tasks.

That why it's important to be thinking actively and in the '-ing' rather than thinking in the '-ed' (as activity done once and closed).

You shouldn't be thinking '-ed' as in qualified, planned, assigned or motivated. You should be thinking qualifying, planning, assigning, motivating, etc. In this way, we recognize that activities are ongoing, ever-changing, fluid and need to be updated as changes occur and new information is received.

It is a naïve proposal person who qualifies an opportunity and makes a decision to pursue it and then not re-qualify it as new information comes in. Inevitably, as a proposal effort gets underway, new information is garnered, both from the client/customer and internally. The qualification/selection decision needs to be reviewed in light of significant new information.

Likewise with other proposal activities: You develop a proposal plan and then you continually adjust and revise that plan. Throughout any proposal development effort the plan will change many times as you adjust for real life coming in to play.

You'll remember that the over-riding purpose of a kick-off meeting is "to inform and motivate". Thereafter, you don't want to think of the team as informed and motivated. You need to be continually informing and motivating the team (I refer to this as "knowing when to hand out the candy bars".)

So, when working on your next proposal development effort, think '-ing', not '-ed'.

--

* Credit for this great tip goes to David Oliver, a member of the Professional Ski Instructor Association's Demo team. He provided this tip during a session I was fortunate enough to attend with him as group leader. Dave pointed out that in skiing, you're never 'ed' and always 'ing'. You're balancing, edging, pressuring, etc. Great tip, Dave!

Daft (Punk) common sense - Jon

I love finding quotes in another context that could have been written about proposals. Take this from the Guardian newspaper earlier in the week, interviewing Thomas Bangalter of dance act Daft Punk:

"The only secret to being in control is to have it [from] the start. Retaining control is still hard but obtaining control is virtually impossible."

He was talking about the media circus surrounding the release of the band's new album – but the same clearly applies to proposals: if you don't get your team working in the right way and to a clear plan from the outset, the project is forever going to be a struggle.

Gold medal kick-offs - Jon

The APMP UK conference last month was an excellent event. Particularly memorable was the keynote speech by Olympic gold medal winning rower Katherine Grainger. Amidst much that was relevant to those of us trying to win business, there was one technique that really caught my imagination.

Before taking gold this summer, Katherine had won silver at three successive Olympics. After Athens (2004), her coach encouraged them to look at every little 'margin of difference' that they could make, to every aspect of their performance, to help them to improve and hence to win.

The result? An improvement on their times – but silver again in Beijing four years later. After that result, they tried a different approach: "we're good enough to be Olympic champions: what could stop us?" – and then worked on those weaknesses, from a position of confidence, capturing glory at London 2012.

I'm going to borrow those techniques for future kick-off workshops, I think. How powerful to routinely ask the team to reflect on:

- what other things could we do – even the smallest changes to the plan and how we work – to maximise our chances of winning?

- we're the best bidder – so what could stop us winning?

Talents and Traits - BJ

Imagine knowing exactly who on your team is the best resource to help solve a particular crisis. Or knowing what personal characteristic of an individual might cause problems 'in the heat of battle'. This is not only possible but essential for a high performing team.

One of my favorite parts of the proposal 'game' is the opportunity to create and work with a successful team. There is certain energy to a group of people who are all performing at a high level and focused on a common set of goals. It's been said that there is nothing more serious than a child at play, and I think a bit of this applies to a proposal team that really has its act together. They're actually *playing*, not working.

I'm often complimented on my ability to help a group of people – very often a diverse set of folks whom I have never met and worked with before – to become a tight unit that functions extremely well together and to do so in a very short time (often in only a day and sometimes in mere hours!)

It is, of course, most flattering to receive such compliments. But the reality is, as with most of the processes I use and suggest, it is not 'rocket science' to create and manage a successful team — it just takes a good solid, logical, common-sense approach.

For each of the proposal engagements I've undertaken over the years, no matter what the size, the steps I've followed have been the same. And here I'd like to highlight one of those steps – that being the uncovering, discussing and understanding of the strengths and the challenges that members bring individually and collectively to the team.

My approach is to have team members present, as the last part of an introduction exercise (and we do an introduction exercise even if everyone knows and has worked with each other), what they see as their talents and their traits. As with each component of the introductions, I frame this very carefully, so that team members will provide the pertinent information.

I start by pointing out that by understanding what each member brings to the team in the way of talent we can, especially when the going gets tough (and it almost always does at some point!), play to that person's strength. The same goes for traits.

Talents

I ask each participant to consider what they bring to the team. I point out that that I'm not looking for academic knowledge or past experience (we've covered this previously in the intros). Here I'm looking for, to put it in sports terms, when they are the 'go-to guy' (using 'guy' generically here of course) for the team.

Perhaps the team member is highly organized and a great planner. Other roles a member might assume are as the 'big picture' person, or the person who knows it's time for everyone to take a break. Maybe he or she can diffuse a tense situation with a bit of humor. All these 'skills' will typically prove to be necessary and valuable in the course of a proposal effort.

--

Traits

Here I ask each person to consider and present, "What about you is going to drive the rest of the team crazy after we've worked with you for three hours, three days or three weeks?"

Team members typically laugh when I ask this – indicating to me that they know exactly what I'm looking for, as well as showing that they're slightly nervous about admitting such things.

I highlight things that typically make others a little nuts – such as the person who is always seeking perfection (to a fault!) or the person who is always late, or perhaps the person who constantly interrupts. Or how about the person who insists on adding his or her two cents, even when the topic doesn't concern them?

By getting such traits on the table and most importantly, by having the person who displays these traits present them and own them, the team can then refer to them without the risk of being the first to point these out. In that way, the team can (hopefully) deal quickly and effectively with the trait and get on with the work, without the embarrassment and associated anger that would typically happen. (Once a trait has been offered up by a team member, referring to it usually provokes humor (and a sheepish, "I know" grin) rather than anger.

--

So next time you're getting your team together – present and discuss the talents and traits each of you brings – and I'm sure you'll find your team is much the stronger for having done so.

Saucy proposal management - Jon

From 'The Oyster House Siege', an entertaining thriller by Jay Rayner (the Observer's restaurant critic), comes the secret for preparing a good Bernaise sauce:

"White wine vinegar, egg yolks, a little butter, and the confidence not to let it know you're afraid."

There's something in that advice. The proposal manager's outlook and disposition have a huge impact on those working on the opportunity: your professionalism and positivity breed professionalism and positivity from those you're leading.

Homework - Jon

I loved an observation made by a senior manager who attended one of my training courses in London last week:

"Too many proposal efforts feel like doing your homework on the bus to school."

Stressful. Rushed. Just good enough not to get into trouble – or get too bad a mark. Yep, I can see the parallels oh so clearly!

In Just Three Words - BJ

I caught a segment on TV that featured people submitting comments in "just three words".

Some were touching – a woman and two children holding a picture of a man in combat gear and a sign with the words "We miss you". Some were humorous – a dog holding a sign that said, "I'll be good". Some were thought provoking: "I'm so scared".

This got me to thinking about what "just three words" statements would come to mind for proposal people.

I'll prime the pump with one of mine – "That was fun!"

In No Uncertain Terms - BJ

I recently worked with a proposal manager whose proposal effort was behind schedule due to missed commitments by members of her team. She had sent out a mail to the team presenting the current status and stating, "I need you to get your pieces to me as soon as possible."

After reading this mail I explained to her that this situation – that she was going to have to miss the deadline and/or submit a poor-quality response – called for a much more direct approach, and that it was time for her to 'swing the bat' (with borrowed authority, in this case from her manager and the CEO, behind it.)

I subsequently wrote a note which I termed an "in no uncertain terms" mail. She tailored this to her project and team and sent it out. I know many of you face similar challenges in getting team members to meet their deliverable dates, so I'm providing the text of my mail.

The text of my "in no uncertain terms" mail:

-

Attention all. We are now in serious jeopardy of missing the deadline and/or submitting an extremely poor-quality proposal due to the significant number of deliverables that are several days past due.

At this point it is highly probable that the response we submit:

- Will present us as being less than competent professionals

- Will not clearly present our solution

- Will not have a clear strategic message

- Will contain incorrect or inaccurate information

- Will be poorly written and contain mistakes

- Will appear to have been written by multiple people rather than one.

Missing the deadlines to which you have committed has directly impacted the overall quality of the response we are developing.

These delays have now necessitated reducing the time available for editing, reviewing, edit/review recovery, printing, assembly, quality control checks, and shipping safeguards — all of which are critical to ensuring the quality of our response.

Failure to address this immediately will cause us to have to miss the deadline as submitting a poor-quality document as described above presents too great a risk to our company.

Your attention to this is required immediately. Please contact me to provide status of your piece and to discuss how we will ensure your deliverables are successfully met.

Respectfully,

--

A warning: This note is intended to be used when the project is really off the rails, not for merely reminding people if they are slightly late. Also, this mail needs to be followed up and it will be ineffective if you let team members 'call your bluff'.

The good news in this particular case is that this client's manager and her CEO both followed up.

The CEO's mail to the team stated, "We ALL agreed that we were going to bid on this project. Bidding does not mean we will forward a half-assed proposal that we are not proud of. I expect everyone to pull their own weight and ensure that we meet our deliverables. If anyone disagrees with this message or feels they cannot comply please let me know immediately."

On deadlines - Jon

A nice quote from Douglas Adams:

"I love deadlines. I like the whooshing sound they make as they fly by."

Reminds me of some proposal contributors I've known over the years.

Leading, not managing - Jon

We've often used the analogy that managing a proposal is like conducting an orchestra.

I've also been known to observe that far too many proposal managers focus far too much on the document and the project plan, rather than on leading the people in the team.

And so I enjoyed the following quote from a recent interview in the Times with soccer manager Andre Villas-Boas, which rather drew the strands together:

"Being a manager is all about emotions. It's about conveying passion, but also about being able to identify how other people feel, and how to be able to deal with that. I remember hearing that there was a maestro from the Boston Philharmonic whose biggest breakthrough was realising that he didn't actually make any sound himself; only his players did. He had to lead them, but he could only do it by harnessing their emotions. The same applies to football managers..."

... and proposal managers, too!

When pigs fly - BJ

There's a shop near my office that has a sign out front which has changeable type, and which has a new message posted every other week or so. I'm sure you know the type of sign to which I'm referring.

99

As I write this, I suppose this might be one of the original forms of 'social media'.

This sign's sayings range from the oft heard, tired and somewhat silly (again, I suspect you know the type) – "My wife ran off with my best friend and boy do I miss him" to simple riddles, occasionally tied to a holiday, as was the case this past Thanksgiving weekend, "Why wouldn't the Pilgrim's pants stay up? His belt and buckle were on his hat."

And occasionally there is a saying that is thought provoking, at least for me (and yes Jon, I do realize that might not take much.)

This week the sign reads, "Given enough thrust, pigs fly just fine."

I like this. There's an underlying message in there. Something about refusing to accept what everyone else believes to be true. Taking on the challenge of the seemingly impossible. Getting the job done despite the odds.

And isn't that what we do on a daily basis? Working on responses where there's not enough time. Having less than ideal and limited resources. Needing to do what others believe can't be done. Hitting both a high standard for quality and a tight deadline. Getting those who would rather not be involved to not only perform but to produce quality work.

So, echoing the sign's sentiment, here's to those of us that figure out how to make pigs fly, and fly pretty damn well in most cases, on a daily basis.

--

* Please note: "No pigs, or any other animals, were harmed in the writing of this post. Further, Strategic Proposals does not suggest, promote nor condone the launching of pigs, or any other animals, or other such attempts to get those animals that are normally earth bound to take flight."

Star (Trek?) proposal teams - Jon

Actor Patrick Stewart has received rave reviews for his performances in Macbeth and Twelfth Night at the Chichester Festival Theatre. I was hugely

100

taken with his behind-the-scenes description of life in the theatre's company, published in the Observer a few weeks back:

"Mostly strangers on day one, the challenges of the play and production have made everyone bolder, braver, vulnerable, needy, self-reliant, co-dependent... By the time the performance begins we are connected, in tune, up, and the experience of each performance is shared, praised, dissected, laughed about at every break and when it is all over."

The parallels with the world of proposals – at its best – are uncanny. As one who's long argued that proposals are primarily a people activity, I'd love to frame this and put it on the desk of every proposal manager. Yet how many of you could honestly say that your proposal teams buzz in the same way as Stewart's company of actors?

First impressions count - Jon

It's so important for a proposal manager to make the right impression with a team from the outset. Turn up late, flustered and unprepared to the kick-off meeting, and you might struggle subsequently to establish an air of professionalism and credibility.

From the participants' perspective, the kick-off is about understanding the opportunity, the process – and their role in it. From a proposal manager's point-of-view, the sub-text is more: "I need you all to be prepared to follow me into battle."

Semi-Autonomous Proposals - BJ

Many of our readers will be aware of, and some of you may even own, a semi-autonomous vehicle.

I've recently purchased one and it's been very interesting adjusting to the vehicle handling some of the driving automatically.

One feature of this new vehicle is the ability to stay within the lane (I call this 'lane lock'). When this feature is engaged, if/as I drift towards one of the lines, the car gives a warning tone and automatically centers itself in the lane.

Another feature is 'adaptive cruise control'. With this feature, I set a certain speed and a number of car lengths to stay behind the vehicle in front of me. So, if I'm doing 65 mph and someone moves in front of me, my vehicle slows down to the same speed as that vehicle and then drops back the designated number of spaces. If the vehicle in front of me slows down, my car slows down. If they stop, my car stops. When they move again, my car moves again. On a recent trip of some 1,000+ miles, I drove without touching the gas pedal or brake, and had to steer only minimally for about 75% of the trip.

Another feature of this vehicle is that when I am low on fuel, the vehicle speaks, in my case in a lovely female voice with a slight British accent, and says, "You have enough fuel to travel approximately 40 miles. Would you like me to locate the necessary service station?" This has proven much more effective than the little light that comes on in my other vehicle (which I inevitably fail to notice until I hear/feel the unmistakable indications of my running out of gas. ;-)

A final feature is that my new vehicle automatically applies the brakes if I am in danger of colliding with something.

So, what's all this have to do with proposals? Driving a semi-autonomous vehicle has had me thinking about what it would be like (what it WILL be like perhaps?) if/when semi-autonomous proposals are a reality.

Suppose there was an application with a feature that kept the developer of content on topic. I'll call this 'topic lock'. While typing away, if/as the writer was veering off topic, they would hear a warning tone and they'd be offered suggestions for getting back on topic...a verbal 'nudge' if you will.

Or perhaps there'd be a feature that prevents the content developer from stating something that was prohibited or would result in disqualification. An applying of the brakes, so to speak.

And as to deadlines and such, imagine if the application were able to notify you of an approaching deadline. The application might speak and say something like,

"Your submission is due in less than 24 hours. Would you like me to request an extension?"

When I first began driving in the late '60s (yes Jon, it was quite some time ago!), the car I had (it was an ancient early '50s Buick) didn't have power brakes, power steering or even seat belts. And now I'm driving a vehicle that handles much of the driving for me.

When I first began working on proposals (in the early '80s) there were no word processors, no spell check, no proposal applications and 'cut and paste' was just that.

At the recent APMP conference I saw proposal applications that automatically formatted documents, identified such things as clichés and overly used words and let the content developer know when they were reaching their allotted word or page count. Perhaps semi-autonomous proposals aren't too far in our future.

"The basis of optimism is sheer terror." - Oscar Wilde

On: executive sponsorship

Ships collide: no-one hurt - Jon

Whilst I was in Japan recently, their navy rather unfortunately crashed a warship into a passing boat. Said latter vessel being rather large, the navy came off worse – and the destroyer caught fire. Fortunately, it wasn't serious, and there were no injuries.

The press reported that the Japanese Prime Minister had been informed of the incident, and had ordered an immediate enquiry. His office confirmed that the PM had also issued orders to naval staff to do everything possible to contain the fire and put it out.

The second part of this rather amused me. I'm picturing the chain of events – a loud crash; flames; a call to the admiral; the message conveyed with urgency to the PM's office. The ratings on the warship standing round confused, wondering what to do as the fire burned furiously...

Eventually, the order arrives back from the PM: "Put out the flames"; the naval officers realise that this is a great idea and rush for the fire extinguishers, saved by the politician's brilliantly perceptive advice.

For Prime Minister, read all too many senior execs when it comes to bids: standing by, letting the flames burn as chaos reigns (with too few staff working too many hours to try to produce the proposal against the odds) – or, more usually, taking credit for a win where their involvement has been (at best) minimal.

The Executive Sponsor - Jon

A recent discussion with a client revolved around the role of the Executive Sponsor on a bid. Whilst I've worked with many such senior figures on deals, I don't think I've ever actually come across – or written – a list of their responsibilities. Here was my quick stab at it:

--

External focus

- Be seen by the customer as the senior manager accountable for the bid – and ultimate successful delivery of the project.

- Drive strategy / plan for contact with senior-level customer contacts / influencers.

- Host / lead / contribute to client events as appropriate (e.g. meetings, visits, presentations).

--

Internal focus

- Actively champion the importance of the opportunity – ensuring it's viewed as a 'will win' deal.

- Ensure relevant senior colleagues are appropriately briefed / consulted regarding the opportunity, and that their views are suitably reflected.

- Qualification: ensure that the deal is properly qualified in, with the resourcing plan fully understood and supported by all at senior levels.

- Secure the involvement of senior colleagues in the bid/proposal effort as required.

- Chair any regular bid/proposal reviews (not daily calls - more occasional overviews)

- Provide active, visible support to the bid/proposal team – supporting with ideas, motivation, etc.

- Act as a point of escalation for any bid/proposal issues, including resourcing problems requiring resolution with / by senior colleagues.

- Participate in formal reviews as required – e.g. Strategy, Storyboard, 'Red Team'.

- Approvals: provide senior-level bid approval – confirmation that the corporation is happy to submit, given clearly stated risks / assumptions, and is doing enough to win.

- Ensure learning points are identified via a Learning Review, and take accountability for reviewing recommended actions and ensuring a clear plan is in place for their implementation.

On: governance and reviews

Stop the red team! - Jon

Just seen a reminder for next week's UKAPMP session. The topic is "Red Team Reviews". I struggle with the very terminology.

Most good proposal writers devote hours to removing unnecessary jargon from their documents, making them as easy as possible for the customer to understand. I can therefore never understand why, as a profession, we seem to revel in creating our own jargon. 'Red team', 'blue team', 'magenta team' (I made that last one up, but I'm sure there's someone out there right now preparing for a Magenta Review Meeting).

It all adds to the mystique of the proposal process, and acts as yet another barrier for salespeople and content contributors – who dislike writing proposals at the best of times. We make them learn an entirely new language before they can even join in! What on earth is wrong with 'Independent Review', 'Peer Review', or some other phrase that stops us hiding behind unnecessary gobbledygook?

And whilst I am being provocative, if the jargonistic title is number one on my list of pet hates, the remainder of my 'top ten common pitfalls' in this area would probably be as follows:

1   Late, inadequate briefing of review participants.

2 Inexperienced (or, perhaps, inappropriately experienced) review participants ("Please read this as if you were the customer. What, you've never evaluated a proposal on the customer side of the table? Oh well, have a go anyway!").

3 Lack of training for review participants. ("Hey, just have a go!")

4 Participants who are too close to the opportunity in question – and who therefore seek to impose their own pre-existing prejudices on the document.

5 The 'red team' (bah, humbug) being the first independent review that takes place. (Far better if you can capture wise ideas from the 'great and the good' early, using outputs from a proper strategy and storyboarding session).

6 Reviews conducted too late, giving too little time for the review itself, and too little time to incorporate any feedback.

7 A poor feedback process. Pity the poor proposal manager, in the dying days of the proposal effort, desperately trying to pull in the final remaining content – and being dragged off to hear the oh-so-superior red team's comments!

8 Confused scope. (There's one leading consultancy out there, who'd better remain nameless, who sees proofreading as a core activity for the 'red team'. Yikes. The people who have the right skills to peer review your document are most certainly not the people you want to be your proofreaders).

9 Excessive internal focus. No matter how hard you try to get the team to review through customer-tinted-spectacles, there's a tendency to default back to analysing the risks to your organisation should you win.

Approval disapproval - Jon

I recently listened in as the person at the next desk led a two-hour approvals meeting, 48 hours before their proposal was due with the customer. I wasn't being nosey – but it's rather tough not to overhear when someone two feet away is bellowing down the phone line to a cast of thousands on the end of a conference call. It was depressing listening, as they argued about whether their financial model and implementation plan were too risky – with nary a mention of the customer or competition.

At the end of the call, she put down the phone in frustration, and turned to a colleague: "They didn't approve it. I'm going to have to cancel my dinner appointment tonight. We need to schedule another approvals board session tomorrow."

And then, to my amazement, she shrugged her shoulders and added: "Then again, I didn't expect them to say 'yes'."

The whole episode served as a microcosm of what's wrong with so many bid approvals processes:

Why so late? A robust process secures in-principle approval early, so that the stakeholders understand the opportunity and their final decision is easy ("are we within the variables we agreed initially?"). Amending the proposal as the result of a late disagreement should be the very, very rare exception – not the rule.

Why so internally focused? If we're testing whether the offer should be amended, doesn't this need to work both ways: are we doing enough to win, as well as whether we'd be happy with the deal as it stands?

Why so many people? "Hey, we've got nothing better to do: let's go and make mischief on a bid". You do want all those who'll be accountable for delivering to stand up and be counted – "we'll make this happen successfully when we win" – but surely there's a cleverer way? Delegated authorities, anyone?

Why so long? Two hours? To sign-off a simple, low-value deal for a standard product?

Why so unsure? The bid team's so lacking in confidence that it's not sure its own management will support them. But the proposal will be fantastic, and their bid presentation will ooze clarity and conviction, right?

So here's the deal. If your final approvals process regularly results in you having to rework your proposal in the final 72 hours, forget what you were planning on doing next, and head straight for your Chief Executive's office once you've finished reading. And don't leave until they've empowered you to change the fundamentally flawed way in which you're having to work.

On: proofreading

Honest Answers - BJ

This following response was sent into us by one our readers.

"ABC company will benefit from our firm's expensive experience in successfully implementing this type of program."

This is an excellent example of a misspelling which spell check wouldn't catch. Or perhaps this response is just extremely honest.

Pedantic - Jon

Are you one of those people who just can't resist looking for errors when reading documents – any documents, not just proposals? Me too! In which case, you might like this – from an Observer restaurant review a couple of weekends back from the marvellous Jay Rayner:

"There used to be a cartoon stuck to the wall of this newspaper's office, mocking the deadening effects of the pedantic subeditor. The sub is leaning over the shoulder of a Victorian chap who is scribbling away with a quill. 'Come, come, Mr Dickens,' the sub is saying, 'it cannot be both the best and the worst of times.'"

Enthusiastic dishonesty? - Jon

Thanks to a friend for sharing her favourite proposal proofreading error... in which a colleague relying on their computer's spellcheck had inevitably failed to pick up on the rather significant difference between the words 'like' and 'lie'.

As in:

"We always lie to satisfy our customers."

Making it up - Jon

My favourite recent example of 'newordology'. One of our associates was proofreading some proposal text recently. The exchange went something like this:

Proofreader: "You can't use 'geoscope'."

Proposal team member: "Why on earth not?"

Proofreader: "Because it's not in the dictionary."

Proposal team member: "But it's a really good way of explaining that we offer worldwide coverage."

Proofreader: "Yes, but it's not a word."

Proposal team member: "Well we like it. Leave it in anyway."

Seeking divine inspiration? - Jon

I've just received a marvellous note from the co-ordinator of a training course we're running next week, about lunch arrangements:

"Just to check – do either of you guys have any deity requirements at all?"

As I explained in my reply, I'm not actually a religious man!

I'll Drink to That! - BJ

I received a mail from someone recently thanking me for my having reviewed and offered advice on his APMP Practitioner Accreditation Questionnaire.

This individual said that my comments and suggested changes had been very helpful and that when incorporated, had resulted in a much stronger questionnaire. They finished by thanking me for, "...imbibing confidence in me."

Though I hadn't suggested that the questionnaire needed so much work this individual should consider turning to the bottle, I guess that's one way to get confidence.

Tears of joy? – Jon

I'm sure we all have our favourite stories of calamitous proofreading errors. The funniest two mistakes I've seen lately, both in the same proposal... a company who had excellent systems in place to enable them to 'detain our staff' (I hope they meant 'retain'), and who classed their customers into three groups depending on the size of the contract – duly named:

Tear 1

Tear 2

Tear 3

I shared these the day after reading them with a group with which I was working. One of those present offered up his own all-time favourite: witnessing an account manager's face as she clicked onto a slide about their company's "Public training courses". Only they didn't quite get all the letters into the word "public"...

Termination Clause - BJ

How about this, for a clause taken from a real-life ITT we reviewed recently:

"10.3 At the end of the Contract all data shall be handed back to the Authority and the Contractor shall be destroyed."

You know, sometimes one probably shouldn't submit a 'fully compliant' response...

Well In Doubt - BJ

I know that many of you, like Jon and I, are avid readers. I also suspect many of you, like us, when lacking for something that we want or need to read, will read whatever happens to be within reach.

I recently found myself reading a local entertainment guide, for lack of anything else to read while eating lunch. It contained a few restaurant reviews, a couple of articles on various community events and a few pages of clubs and music venues. And it also had a personals section at the back.

Within a few minutes I had read all the articles, skimmed through the listings and found myself reading the personal ads (purely out of having nothing else to read I assure you).

Under 'couples for couples', I came across an ad that made me laugh out loud and which clearly demonstrates the need for the services of someone with the right skills set, in this case an editor.

This personal ad read,

"Married couple seeks same. Woman must be pretty, sexy and sensual. Man must be muscular, handsome and well in doubt."

Either this couple is seeking an insecure guy or this is a great example of the often-humorous effects of the misuse of words.

That number again is... - BJ

While sharing war stories, a participant in a recent workshop, Christina, told the group of the dangers associated with trying to do things from memory and not writing them down.

Christina said she had memorized several company numbers and didn't bother to look them up when putting them into a proposal.

After submission, she learned from the client that she had apparently transposed the last four digits of the company's 800 phone number. Fortunately, this client was laughing when he called to tell her that the response he received when he called the number was a bit surprising. The person who answered asked him, "Have you been a bad boy? Is that why you've called the Spank Me line?"

I'm sure this will act as a reminder for us all to double check the numbers in the proposals we submit. (I'm pretty sure Christina won't need reminding in the future.)

Don't Go There! - BJ

OK, when developing a document and waiting for specific information (a date, name, link, etc.) it is fairly standard practice to put in a 'marker' where the information is to be inserted once it is known. This typically takes the form of xx/xx/xx, or insert XXX here.

Using this method, you'd use logically www.XXX.com to indicate a link, right? The intention, of course, is that these be filled in before submitting the document and ideally (and as we teach our clients), these are highlighted to ensure that in fact they are filled in prior to submission and NOT overlooked.

However, as we all know, despite all best efforts (or for lack of them!), once in a great while that doesn't always happen and one of these ends up in the final document as is.

Very unfortunately, that's just what happened recently: A document went out with www.XXX.com in it. As you might have guessed, though unbeknownst to the person who quite innocently used this as a marker, this is actually a working link. And like the title says, it's not a link to which you want to be directing your client. (And I strongly suggest you DON'T GO THERE!)

"In certain kinds of writing… it is normal to come across long passages which are almost completely lacking in meaning." - George Orwell

On: proposal presentations

The Olympic ideal - Jon

Somewhat at the last moment, I was handed the honour of opening last week's UKAPMP conference in Bournemouth with my presentation on 'The Proposal Top Ten', in which I helped the audience to benchmark their proposal capabilities.

I was followed onto the stage by David Magliano, Marketing Director for the winning 2012 London Olympic bid. Of all his fascinating anecdotes, what really stuck in my mind was the preparation that went into the team's final presentation to the Olympic decision-makers. London had six speakers, each talking for three minutes. In case one of these fell ill, they'd also lined up a substitute who could jump in to replace any of the six (putting across the same key messages, but swapping in their own personal anecdotes for those of the original speaker).

The team leaders had watched the tape libraries to study every single presentation from the previous twelve years of Olympic bids. They created a replica of the presentation suite, so the speakers were familiar with the set-up in advance.

By the time they presented, they'd reached version 35 of the script. They'd had 10 rehearsals as a group, and each speaker had 20 hours of individual coaching.

Now, most of us aren't involved in bids of that scale, and couldn't afford to invest the time or costs associated with that degree of planning. But it does throw down a challenge – are your bid teams rehearsing their presentations, or simply turning up and hoping that it'll be all right on the day?

Sales techniques - Jon

An amusing evening recently with a small group of very senior salespeople, who shared their favourite stories from their bidding career.

The first anecdote concerned a bid to a major Japanese institution. During the pitch, it became obvious that many of the client team didn't speak especially good English, or really understand the complex solution under discussion. So the bid team started to introduce fictitious information into their explanations. Amongst the financial regulations and indices that would affect the deal were four that were particularly important: 'R2', 'D2,' 'C3' and 'PO'...

And then there were the days in which financial houses could pretty much name their price for services to ill-informed clients. One offer included an 'administration fee' – equivalent, effectively, to pure profit for the bidder, with little actual justification.

So, how to fix the amount? Here's the game they played in some London meetings: look out of the window, spot the number of the third bus to pass, and go with that. If the number 9 bus went past, the admin fee was £9,000; pity the client on the day it was route 141...

Closing the doors - Jon

My travels for work took me to Brittany last month – a great group for the course, in a lovely part of the world. I had work to do most evenings, but writing whilst overlooking a picturesque harbour certainly beat being in the office!

I was staying in a small, family-run hotel: clean, comfortable but a little basic. I arrived at 9pm on the first evening of my stay, and the ever-so-friendly receptionist gave me a code for the front door – 'just in case' I needed it. I dropped my bags in my room, set straight off for dinner – and returned an hour or so later to find the hotel in darkness, the front door locked. Thank goodness I'd remembered the code – and thank goodness my plane hadn't been delayed on the way in!

So here's a debate: when does – and when should – your proposal centre 'lock its door' on a bid on which you've been working?

Many proposal teams engage with the sales team purely up to the moment at which a document is delivered. Some recognise the value of staying engaged until the team presents the proposal to the customer. Many support the bid effort throughout endless rounds of clarification and negotiation, struggling to disengage and even risking being dragged into transition and delivery!

In our desire to be helpful and to win business, there's definitely a danger that some proposal folks stay involved too long. Certainly, salespeople will try to keep you on board for as long as they can: after all, you make their lives easier. But we're not there as comfort blankets for account managers or for the team who are responsible for designing and implementing your offer.

The optimal point of disengagement depends – to an extent – on the skillset within your team, on where you can add the most value with the capacity / headcount you have available, and on the definition and perception of your role within the business.

For me, the default 'door shutting' moment for a proposal team is after the proposal presentation – I think the continuity that we bring at such a critical stage, helping to translate the written book into a powerful presentation and helping to coach and rehearse the team, are hugely important. But after that? It's time to lock the door and give the salesperson the code for use in emergencies.

After I'd stumbled through the front door of the hotel after dinner in near-total darkness, searching in vain for a light switch and struggling up the stairs to my room, I also reflected that there are good ways and bad ways of handling the proposal team's disengagement from the bid. You need to communicate clearly up front, and then to handle your exit professionally and in line with expectations – you don't want to leave the team with whom you've been working feeling suddenly unloved, or thinking that you're abandoning them!

Save the last dance for me - Jon

I recently read some interesting academic research on the correlation between the order in which candidates appear in a contest, and the likely result. I'm not sure whether it applies directly to the world of bids and proposals, but it's certainly given me some food for thought.

Wändi Bruine de Bruin of Carnegie Mellon University has written a couple of papers now on the theme 'Save the last dance for me'. She's studied the outcomes of figure skating competitions and the Eurovision Song Contest (!), and also reviewed other research into contests as varied as gymnastics, classical music and synchronized swimming.

The results aren't entirely clear cut, but some strong patterns do emerge which tend to back up our 'last or first' philosophy.

Broadly speaking, if candidates are judged via a step-by-step approach – that is, each individual entrant is scored and discussed immediately after they've taken their turn – then the data suggests that it's better to go last since "contestants who performed later in the sequence generally received better scores".

Judges compare each performance to its predecessors and "tend to overweigh the unique features of each new, focal, performance". However, if an 'end-of-sequence' procedure is used, where "judges do not announce their scores until all contestants have performed", "one may expect judges to give higher scores to contestants that are remembered better. Research on free recall suggests that first and last appearing options are more likely to be remembered."

Fascinating stuff: I'd love to see some research into bid presentations. Then again, proper planning, an effective content design process for the presentation, development of great collateral, a properly managed rehearsal and careful choreography of the logistics all probably play a bigger part in improving your chances of success than the order in which you happen to present!

"There's no such thing as a nice surprise in a bid presentation." - Kevin Treeby, Director of Procurement, House of Commons – 'Altitude' proposal conference, chaired by Jon in London, 2009

On: learning reviews

Learning reviews are a waste of time - Jon

Well, they shouldn't be, of course. But the sad reality is that (from the perspective of the proposal team, at least), they usually fail to lead to any real change.

Debating this with a client in Germany shortly before Easter, I came up with a list of four disconnects that act as barriers in the process for lost deals – even if a review does take place.

First, there's the disconnect between the real reasons why a vendor lost and the story that buyer tells the salesperson. So much easier as a buyer to send the account team away with "you lost on price" (and hence aren't personally to blame) than to tell the whole truth.

Second, there's the disconnect between whatever the buyer tells the salesperson, and the spin that the salesperson feeds back to their organisation. There's a degree of self-protection at play, resulting in sanitised messages and "it wasn't my fault".

Third, there's the disconnect between the messages the salesperson feeds back, and any learning specifically about the quality of the proposal. It's vital for the organisation to know about pricing, solution quality and suchlike. But the proposal team need to know what the buyer thought of the document itself (and how it compared to those of their competitors), and these topics are rarely discussed.

And finally, there's the disconnect between the outcomes of the review and the actions that should result. I can often look back over a dozen learning reviews that an organisation has conducted over the past six months, to find that they all show the same fundamental causes – yet nothing substantive has been done. If you don't schedule the follow-up checkpoints with someone with clout – to take place (say) three months later – nothing will happen.

The third learning review - Jon

The APMP syllabus would, quite rightly, have us believe that a proposal team should conduct two internal learning review (or 'lessons learnt') sessions.

The first should take place soon after submitting the document – whilst the team's views are still fresh in their minds. Key topics for debate include identifying what the team did well (i.e. techniques and tactics that should be repeated on future deals), as well as what could have been improved (by individuals, or systemically by the organisation).

Customers then often take forever to make their purchasing decision – prevaricating for weeks and months, often going through an exhaustive process of clarification and negotiation. And even once they've appointed their chosen supplier, it may not be appropriate to seek detailed feedback on your proposal until the dust has settled, or until (if you've won the deal) implementation is safely underway. The prevailing 'best practice' would therefore be that the team needs to revisit their learning once they've captured the customer's feedback – again, a sound principle to follow.

It strikes me that there should probably be a third learning review, say twelve months after you've won a deal. Too often, when projects are delivered, they fail to meet the customer's expectations or the supplier's goals; the two organisations' respective teams struggle to make sense of what was documented and agreed during the bid process. Perhaps it's a case of "It doesn't do what it says on the can", or maybe simply "We hadn't fully understood or anticipated that".

Understanding whether this has been the case is critical – and diagnosing anything that could have been done differently in the bid or proposal to prevent the issues from occurring strikes me as crucial. And for those projects that are a resounding success? Again, clear assessment of what went well – and communication of why this was – could add huge value to the organisation.

I thought it was a fascinating point, and it's one I think I'll emphasise rather more in future when working with teams who are looking to learn and to improve. Let's call it 'the birthday review'. I wonder if it'll catch on?

Learning from the good stuff

Presenting an APMP Foundation Level training course before Christmas, I found myself getting frustrated by the negative spin that the examiners take on the learning reviews. What's the point, according to the syllabus, of a lessons learned process? It's to "recognize systemic process issues and drive their resolution"; the aim is "to do better next time".

It struck me that whoever developed this section of APMP's competency framework must have had some pretty bad personal experiences running proposals. If the learning review is so negative – working from the assumption that so much went on that was wrong, that so many things need to be corrected – then it's no wonder that it can be hard to secure people's open, frank participation in the process. The working assumption would appear to be that the proposal team has just endured a soul-destroying journey into the valley of despair – and the inevitable risk is that those who do participate in the learning process will approach the exercise feeling defensive, confrontational and negative.

No! A learning review should be framed in a positive way. Look to celebrate what went well on the bid – those things you'd do again; the things that worked; the things you'd want other teams to try on their next proposal effort.

And then – without attributing blame – look at what the team would have done differently (with the benefit of hindsight, perhaps), or would want to approach in a different way the next time around. After all, even the most successful bids aren't all plain sailing – and so many unsuccessful teams do so much cool stuff without quite getting across the finishing line in first place.

Interesting, but not necessarily correct – Jon

Dinner in a Parisian restaurant recently; there's a notice pinned to a box on the wall:

"Your comments interest us."

I love that they're curious to hear what you think; that they'll weigh up what you say and – in the refreshing underlying implication of the message – that they may well conclude that whilst you are entitled to your opinion, it may be entirely wrong.

Feedback on proposals – from customers or team members – is always fascinating to hear. Yet, of course, it's not always correct, fair – or, necessarily, honest: people do play games to protect their own position, avoid conflict, transfer blame, claim credit, seize the moral high ground, dodge further actions.

It's why strong, impartial facilitation of these debriefs and workshops is so important.

Everyone comes second - Jon

You know what happens. Your sales team have just sought feedback on the deal they've just lost. They come back from meeting the client, bearing news that's not as disastrous as they'd feared. "They told us we came a very close second. They said our proposal was really great." More often or not they add: "It really just came down to price."

It always amazes me how many teams 'come second' in any particular procurement exercise. There must be a lot of silver medals waiting to be handed out in buyers' desk drawers.

It always amazes me how many losing teams submitted proposals that were 'really great'. So great they contributed to losing the deal.

And it always amazes me how many losing teams submitted the best solution, with the top team, but were thwarted 'on price' even though the client had complete faith that their approach was by far the best.

In reality, of course, it's not like that. The customer offering feedback – if indeed they can be bothered doing so – is focused on avoiding challenge, letting the losing team hold their heads a little higher, and hoping that somehow this might result in a better offer next time round. They're offering kind words, not scathing critiques.

There's another challenge, too, very apparent to me when I'm coaching folks through APMP's Foundation Level qualification. There's a detailed checklist in the association's training pack, with eight questions to use in the client debrief. They're all very valid issues, covering ease of evaluation, compliance and more.

Yet my experience when I ask people emerging from client debriefs is that the proposal is last on their list in those discussions. "What did they say about our proposal?" "We were 2.3% out on price."

"And about the document we sent them?"

"They didn't like that we weren't compliant with clause 28.2 of their Ts & Cs. And they thought the project manager we put forward was a bit too junior."

(Me, getting frustrated): "But what about the quality of our document – developed at the expense of so much blood, sweat and tears?"

"Oh: sorry. I ran out of time to ask them about that."

And, you know, I'd probably agree that in the limited time available, gathering feedback on your proposition is probably more important than on your proposal and pitch. If your products and services, implementation or legal approaches, costs and prices, are consistently out of kilter with the market leaders, it's critical to understand that. Clients are going to want to discuss that. And, practically, nobody getting a debrief is going to get time to ask all of APMP's eight proposal-related questions.

My preference in practice therefore is to focus the team seeking feedback on a couple of simple linked questions – such as "how did our proposal documents compare to those from our competitors", then "...and what about our presentation?".

Then, away from the battle, a client audit – with selected recipients of proposals in (say) the past quarter – is the perfect mechanism for a deeper dive. An interview (face-to-face if possible) by someone with a degree of independence from the team involved in the bid might take half an hour of the client's time.

And so much the better if that uses a structured form, allowing the buyer to give your documents and presentations a comparative score versus the best of the other bidders – as well as to provide comments. The learning that results from this, done well, is so incredibly useful that I find it amazing that it's not an approach adopted by more proposal teams – indeed, by all proposal teams.

On: lawyers

Confidential - BJ

Yes. Best practice does say that there should be a legal disclaimer, highlighting the confidentiality of the proposal's content and how the information may or may not be distributed, used, copied, etc. However, if this is overdone, it can leave the person reviewing your document feeling as if they've been put in hand cuffs.

Witness the following disclaimer from an e-mail received by one of our associates. Only the company name and information has been changed. As the saying goes, you can't make this stuff up folks. If you've seen one that's even longer, send it along (with a generic name inserted, of course.)

--

The information contained in this E-Mail and any subsequent correspondence is private and is intended solely for the intended recipient(s). The information in this communication may be confidential and/or legally privileged. Nothing in this e-mail is intended to conclude a contract on behalf of ABC Company or make ABC Company subject to any other legally binding commitments, unless the e-mail contains an express statement to the contrary or incorporates a formal Purchase Order.

For those other than the recipient any disclosure, copying, distribution, or any action taken or omitted to be taken in reliance on such information is prohibited and may be unlawful.

Emails and other electronic communication with ABC Company may be monitored and recorded for business purposes including security, audit and archival purposes. Any response to this email indicates consent to this.

Telephone calls to ABC Company may be monitored or recorded for quality control, security and other business purposes.

ABC Company Registered in the USA, the UK and Europe: Company I.D. Number: AW231953RTF390495SRDW, Address: 123 Any Street, Somewhere, State, 90454-39453, United States of America. Ship to address: ABC Company, Post Office Box 435-23432, State, 90454-39453. Phone: 234-567-8901. Hours of operation 8-5, Mon-Fri, EST.

www.anycompany.com

info@anycompany.com

This e-mail and any attachments are for authorized use by the intended recipient(s) only. It may contain proprietary material, confidential information and/or be subject to legal privilege. It should not be copied, disclosed to, retained or used by, any other party. If you are not an intended recipient then please promptly delete this e-mail and any attachment and all copies and inform the sender. Thank you.

From a legal perspective... - Jon

Any of you suffer from paranoid corporate lawyers? Too often, legal disclaimers create entirely the wrong impression at the outset of the document – the sort of thing which, when paraphrased, probably reads to the customer as:

"We do not trust you. We think you will steal our ideas. And no matter how much this document talks about 'partnership', remember that our legal team are always lurking menacingly in the shadows."

I thought you might enjoy two recent examples encountered by our UK team.

First up, an ITT question: "Please indicate your process for responding to proposals or quotations." The answer, submitted to the proposal team by their company lawyer: "We do not provide quotations or proposals".

And then the disclaimer at the front of a different document:

"This document is not an offer, nor does any part of it represent an offer and nor does anything which may be construed as an offer constitute an offer of any form."

The simple copyright statement provides you with so much legal protection. But if you are pressured to include anything more, why not make it more friendly by adopting a mutual stance:

"Just as we have treated the information that you have provided to us as confidential, we trust you will do the same with the material we have included in this proposal. Thank you."

On: procurement

The festive season? - Jon

Two questions on my mind, as I start back at work in 2014: what proportion of proposal people ended up working on bids over the festive season - and why on earth are very many procurement people so disrespectful of the staff working for their suppliers as to set deadlines at the very start of January?

I can offer my own perspective on the latter, from my days in purchasing (before I switched sides of the negotiating table, back in 1999). Running a very large (multi-hundred-million pound) global outsourcing deal for a major bank, our project plan included the eminently reasonable target of completing our RFP by the end of the year – before we broke for Christmas and the New Year.

What we then did surprised the shortlisted vendors: once the document was finalised (around the 18th, if I recall correctly), we refused to send it to them. Our rationale?

Firstly, that we wanted the bid teams to be fresh and creative when preparing their responses. And secondly that expecting people to work over the holidays was entirely inconsistent with our stated aims of genuinely finding a 'partner' who could help us to bring about change to the way in which services were delivered to our organisation.

That's why our project plan was always clear: complete the RFP before the holidays; issue it at the very start of January, and then give the bidders sufficient time to respond professionally. Good for them – but, ultimately, helping to draw out the best propositions from the market for us.

I rather suspect that's an unusual approach for a procurement manager to take – but, then again, this was a somewhat unusually forward-looking and strategic purchasing function, many of whose members have gone on to do other wonderful things in their careers since.

Your more typical – junior, tactical, arrogant buyer – is far less likely to care, or even to think through the consequences (for them!) of their actions when issuing a Yuletide document.

So, if you're in a part of the world where this has been a holiday season, did you end up working flat out right through the end of December, or heading straight back into the office on the morning of 1st January? And, do you think the potential clients concerned got the very best of your organisation in the offer and proposal that you submitted as a result?

Editing Gone Wild - BJ

While editing a response to an RFP, I came upon a paragraph which was very poorly written, unclear and needed a complete rewrite.

I did just that. I took the time to understand what the paragraph was really trying to say. I then rearranged the order of the information, restructured several of the sentences and completely rewrote others. When I was done, I would say, at the risk of sounding conceited, that the paragraph was much clearer and easier to understand, and it was written well and correctly.

It was only after I had completed this exercise that I realized the paragraph was part of the RFP and not the response. As Charlie Brown would say, "Arrrrgggh!"

Maybe this has happened to you. You have become so caught up in editing or worked with an RFP that was so poorly written, that you've inadvertently edited the RFP itself. Please tell me I'm not the only one who's done this. (And yes, sadly, this is not the first time it's happened to me.)

I would point out that anyone who has a bit of time in the proposal game has surely come across an RFP that was poorly written and very unclear. Such RFPs, and the one I've described above in particular, would have benefited greatly from some of Jon's expertise in developing effective RFPs. As he's said many a time to a buyer (and this is also the name of a course Jon presents), "You get the response you deserve."

The fear factor - Jon

Steve Mullins, a dear friend – and one of the leading lights in the world of procurement – made the following lovely observation when we were chatting the other day:

"What's the scariest phrase for a buyer to hear after selecting their supplier?"

"What a brave decision!"

I love this. I well recall from my own procurement days that, whilst we focused on what good would look like, the flipside was always a concern: what if this went wrong? Can you imagine a buyer saying any of the following?

- I want to have to work really, really hard personally to make this work.

- I don't mind my users shouting at me.

- I don't mind my bosses shouting at me.

- If it's late, who cares….?

- Unexpected extra costs? I don't mind going to ask for more money.

- Bring on the excitement – I love surprises!

I doubt it. And it re-emphasises the need to think about the customer's hopes and – especially – fears when formulating your proposal strategies.

'The Buyer's Guide to Bidding' - Jon

A survey of senior figures in the proposal world, led by Jon and Steve Mullins – one of the most esteemed figures in the world of procurement – generated some fascinating quotes. Here's a top ten:

1 "A good written proposal, in itself, might not win you business but a badly conceived and written one may put you out of the race."

2 "It is never enough to say, "I'm qualified." So is everyone else. The point is "Pick me because I'm different.""

3 "The easier the seller makes it for us the better for them."

4 "Some proposals are articulate, really have got under my skin, are really convincing – whereas others look mechanical, dull, pre-written and could have been meant for anyone."

5 "They vary from excellent (rare) to awful (quite common), but most of them are mediocre."

6 "Your ability to do what is required of you at proposal stage reflects upon your ability to perform once in contract!"

7 "Buyers are not idiots. They read good proposals thoroughly and they are not amused at fluff, being patronised, inconsistency, arrogance or shabby editing."

8 "Buyers are seeking a reasonable deal with low risk to themselves (oh yes, and their employer!)."

9 "Clearly understand the problem to be solved. Then and only then can you provide the appropriate solution."

10 "If the customer wants the responses written in quill, printed on papyrus with a bow around it, please conform. Comparing proposals that don't follow the templates requested is often a long and difficult task… and does lower the tolerance levels of those marking."

The buyer's hopes and fears - Jon

What's it like being a purchaser? As regular readers will know, I started my career in procurement before moving into the world of proposal management – and I still spend a fair proportion of my time with buyers and evaluators. I thought a few insights into life on the other side might be of interest:

1 The enemy lies within. Somewhat bizarrely, the easiest discussions for a buyer are with their potential suppliers. It's far tougher trying to align resources, budgets and views internally. Running the procurement process is often a precarious high-wire act.

2 Powerless purchasers. The evaluation team will formulate recommendations as to which supplier to choose – but they'll rarely sign off the decision. Making the presentation internally to the 'great and the good' can be a daunting prospect. And, as a buyer, I'll probably choose whichever bidder I think I can sell internally most easily.

3 "I'm the buyer. Stupid." Most procurement people are acutely conscious that they know far less about the subject matter of the bid than their potential suppliers. (If this is what their organisation did, they wouldn't need to ask you to do it for them!).

4 "Your fate is in my hands." I have the power of life or death over your bid. Win, and you'll get the glory and our money. So you bidders had better be grateful, respectful, deferential and nice to me. (After all, my colleagues internally aren't!).

5 I'll have to live with the consequences of the decision as to which bidder we choose – and those we reject. Thinking short-term, I'll select whichever company will make me hit my performance objectives, whatever they may be. And in the medium term, I'll want the bidder who'll minimise the risk of things going wrong and maximise the probability of me looking like a hero. (And, incidentally, debriefing unsuccessful suppliers can be a terrifying prospect – especially losing incumbents).

6 Making it up as I go along. Only a small minority of purchasers have ever been trained in writing RFPs and leading evaluation workshops. I'll copy and paste, I'll use the last document I wrote; it was probably good enough then, and it'll probably get me through now.

The world's most annoying sign - Jon

I've been working recently in an office that displays a notice prominently in the restrooms, stating:

"Please leave these toilets as you would wish to find them."

Every time I go in, I wish I'd remembered to bring a pot of paint, some nice fluffy towels and a bottle of Molton Brown handwash.

So, I wondered: what's the equivalent irritating phrase in the world of proposals? For me, it has to be the RFP instruction that runs something like:

"Please submit 4 (four) copies of your proposal."

'Cos I didn't realise that "4" meant "four", you know... Procurement folk so often seem to get hide behind pseudo-legalese, thinking it makes them sound clever – when in fact it merely serves to underline how little training they have in developing effective RFPs that entice their prospective vendors to submit the best possible proposals.

The woeful state of public sector procurement - Jon

I think my mission in life for the year ahead [2014] ought to be to destroy public sector procurement as it now functions in the UK.

The job of buying on behalf of government? I have no idea if there's a grand, centrally held mission statement somewhere in Whitehall, or in town halls across the nation. But were I to have a go at drafting it at my desk early on Saturday morning before my first coffee of the day, it'd read something like:

"Professionally sourcing solutions from the market that enable the most effective and most efficient delivery of public services to those who depend on them."

It should be about drawing out excellent offers via excellent proposals from competent bidders, in a well-managed, fair and cost-effective way. As founder of a business, I'd like to hope it helps smaller and local businesses (and disadvantaged groups) to thrive.

As a taxpayer – both personally and through our company – I'd also hope it would be about ensuring value for money: not necessarily the cheapest (for cheap is rarely cheerful), but the option that delivers the best overall use of scarce public funds. That has to be a holistic view – not just the costs billed by the eventual supplier, but factoring in the time and cost of those on the government side of the procurement and delivery too.

To give just a few illustrations of how the inept cadre of so-called procurement 'professionals' operate right now in the UK public sector, from deals we've worked on in the past few months:

- Numerous local councils across the country needing to replace a supplier that's quitting the market, each conducting entirely separate procurement exercises in parallel; each developing their own (typically very second-rate) ITT with different specs and questions about what is fundamentally a very simple commodity purchase.

- A major government department issuing 300 pages of questions for a contract worth under £1m – and for which there are already robust and toughly negotiated framework agreements in place that they could have used.

- Documents issued to bidders in late December, with a response date in early January, with the added fun that clarification questions couldn't be answered until a couple of days before proposals were due in "because everyone's on holiday".

- A project that has huge implications for a local community, being awarded purely on the basis of the short written proposal that bidders are required to submit, with no meetings whatsoever between the agency concerned and potential suppliers to discuss their proposed approaches.

- Laughable word-count limits on answers in eTendering systems. Because, you know, it's obviously possible for a supplier to explain in full how a highly sensitive service protecting the most vulnerable people in our society can be delivered from a technical perspective within the 250-word box you've provided – especially when the question you've posed is itself three pages long and itself contains numerous contradictions and errors.

- Bids on which several suppliers score "100% for quality". Utter nonsense: I'm not sure I've ever seen a truly perfect proposal, not least when the buying teams aren't that clear or realistic about what's needed for success and their RFPs are so badly written. But, hey, if we're not bright enough to differentiate between potential solutions, let's lazily score them all high and just argue about price.

- An eProcurement system that offers two settings: the 'standard view', and an 'alternative view' for the visually impaired. Praiseworthy, save for the fact that the way of making the ITT easier to respond to for the visually impaired is simply to leave the question numbers on the screen but delete all of the questions. You really couldn't make it up.

- Duplicating and wasting effort. Running ridiculously complex processes that merely seem to protect or generate jobs for civil servants. Treating the supply market with contempt. And, as a result, no doubt resulting in poorer public services for those who depend on them, and wasting taxpayers' money. Who's in control of this stuff? And is it any wonder that if things are done so very badly on smaller and medium-sized projects, we hear tell of so many disasters on major procurement exercises?

--

Actually, I'm not sure I blame the individuals: when ineptitude is so widespread, it has to be the system to blame – the very role of the purchasing function; the processes it follows; the calibre of staff recruited (partly tied into the salaries and grades for the job); the training offered; the way feedback from the market is handled.

Of course, it's easy to pick on isolated examples of poor practice – and this post is designed to be provocative: something of 'A Modest Proposal'. There are, of course, many incredibly diligent, top-class procurement folks working in the public sector. But life for them must be very lonely.

"The role of the proposal? Making it easier for the customer to make a 'yes' decision." - Martin Webb – Fellow of the Chartered Institute of Procurement & Supply

On: improving proposal capabilities

That's how we've always done it - BJ

I recently heard a story which caused me to reflect on what Jon and I often see as to the way in which many proposal groups function. I don't know if this story is an urban myth but even if it is, the moral remains the same and, for me at least, delivers an important reminder as to how and why processes are developed and followed.

A newly married couple was hosting a family gathering and they were serving a ham. While they were preparing the ham, the husband informed his wife that his mother had always cut off the two ends of the ham. When asked why the ends were cut off, he said he didn't know but that both his mother and grandmother always served it that way.

Later, when his mother arrived they inquired as to why she had cut off the ends of the ham. The mother admitted she didn't know, but confirmed that her mother had always served ham that way.

The wife surmised that the ham ends were trimmed off because they might be a bit tough and less desirable. The husband guessed it might have been because it made for crispier end pieces. The mother offered that her mother might have done this because it caused the ham to cook a bit faster. They all agreed the ends might have been cut off merely for appearance's sake as it made the ham look more uniform.

When the grandmother arrived, the group asked her about the family tradition of cutting off the ends of the ham. In response, looking a bit puzzled she stated, "I don't know anything about a family tradition, but I do know I always had to cut off the ends of a large ham in order for it to fit in my oven as it was very small."

I've no doubt that this relates to a process that might be in place and being followed, even if the reasons for doing so aren't obvious and no one is sure why or if the process is necessary.

137

Burning the midnight oil - Jon

It's always great when we can persuade a senior executive to drop into one of our courses to add their weight to the discussions. Hearing a Chief Executive or Senior Vice President discussing the importance of proposals – and offering their personal support for improvement initiatives – does wonders for the confidence of the attendees.

Only, it doesn't always quite work, no matter how carefully the exec's been briefed. Take the following 'praise' offered to a group of proposal managers at a recent event:

"You guys do a fantastic job – I come up late at night and there you are."

Noooooo! That's precisely what proposal centres should be trying to avoid!

When the security guard on the night shift drops by your desk to say goodnight before heading home – when success is measured in terms of hours worked, commitment viewed as a willingness to persevere with too few resources and an unnecessarily inefficient process – then it's time for change.

Juicy Joe opens his doors - Jon

I'm writing this at just after seven in the morning in central London. I'm relaxing in a comfortable chair, listening to Louis Armstrong, sipping a freshly made 'Iron Man' juice (strawberry, kiwi and apple, since you ask).

I'm running a course this morning, see, and as always arrived at the venue a little early. 'Joe and the Juice' is a couple of doors away – and I'm customer number three. Ever. Today's their first day of operation. And I'm watching as the six staff get set up.

The guy in the pink shirt's just come in with a selection of trendy magazines from the newsagent next door, setting them out for customers to read. A chap in a coat is checking that a colleague knows how to work the juicing machine. A lady in black's chopping fruit. The boss is proudly taking photos. The pride, enthusiasm and anticipation are palpable.

And I wondered... What would your proposal operation look like if you could start from scratch? How many staff would you need, with what skills and attitude? What equipment would you have, and what would your working environment be like? How would you work together – to produce really great results that surprise and delight a growing customer base? What would be playing on the soundtrack?

I won't pretend that you'll be able to make your vision come to life – but if you don't take time to dream, how can you ever start to move on from wherever your team is today to open the doors to the way you'd really like to be able to work?

'Common Sense' and the 'Science' of Proposals - BJ

When presenting proposal concepts, I often speak of or refer to the 'science' of proposals and the 'laws of physics' as they apply to proposals. By these I am referring to the basic, fundamental principles I consider to be the basis of good proposal practice.

These include such mind-expanding concepts as, "In order for a proposal to be well written, the proposal team must have good, solid writing skills." I know, I know. A huge 'duh!' statement, right?

Ok, then how about, "In order to honor quality, it is critical to understand how many proposals it is possible to produce in a specified period of time, given finite resources – including time."

Ok, here too another statement that is so obvious it does not merit mentioning, or does it? How about, "Availability is not a skill." Too obvious? Not in my experience with a great number of clients. Actually, these statements are often real eye openers and lead to significantly changed thinking and behaviors.

Those of you who have seen me present know that we often lead with the Mark Twain quote, "It seems to me that common sense isn't all that common." I believe this is true. Or perhaps I'd spin it a bit and say that common sense seems to often get lost in the heat of battle, over time or just due to lack of attention.

Head for the hills - Jon

I clipped a story from the papers recently about grandee 1960s prime minister Harold Macmillan. His grandson recalled a meeting at the family home. Cabinet colleague 'Rab' Butler produced a pile of papers.

"What are those?" asked Macmillan.

"Policies," said Butler.

"Oh, I beg you, not policies," the prime minister retorted. "They come back to haunt you. Give them broad sunlit uplands, dear boy."

I smiled at the similarity between political spin and the challenge of securing sponsorship from 'on high' for programmes to deliver improvements to proposal capabilities.

As proposal folks, we may be absolutely fascinated by the detail of how we're going to improve our processes, our structures, our documents. Yet when talking to the CEO or Sales Director, we need to remind ourselves that the key to success is to paint a picture of the "broad sunlit uplands" if we want to capture their imagination and support. And budget and headcount!

Look after the pounds - Jon

We have an idiom in the UK that one should: "look after the pennies, and the pounds will look after themselves"

This loosely translates as "if you look after your money carefully, you'll get rich."

It struck me recently that the opposite probably holds true for proposal centres.

Looking after the pennies? That suggests that your senior management are continually looking to shave money from your proposal operations. It'll be an uphill battle to secure investment ("travel's frozen, we've needed a new printer for months, and we can't get funding for training").

It'll all be about improving efficiency, rather than effectiveness. Your energies will be diverted away from trying to win, in favour of trying to economise, to cut corners and to "make the most of a bad job". And the quality of your proposals – and hence your win rates – will inevitably be being compromised.

You need to find a sponsor who "looks after the pounds, rather than worrying about the pennies." Focus your senior executives on the revenue (and margin) improvement opportunities that will derive from improving your proposals, rather than on the penny-pinching. They'll probably only need to win one extra deal per year to pay back any investment you could dream of requesting.

Getting control - Jon

Some organisations' approach to proposals can best be described as 'Disorganised chaos'. Yet it's only two steps from there to being in control:

Disorganised chaos.

Organised chaos.

Organised.

Where are you on the journey?

Improving scores - BJ

The dentist I've been seeing for years has retired, and the new one's using technologies and methods that are new to me.

One such method this new dentist uses is a scoring system for the health of my gums. Some of you will no doubt be familiar with a dentist probing 'pockets' around each tooth. A pocket is an indicator of how healthy gums are, with a healthy pocket being very shallow and problem areas being deeper.

My previous dentist would do this and then typically tell me I need to floss more often or pay better attention to a particular area of my mouth.

When I first visited her about three months ago this new dentist did such a probing and associated scoring. She then showed me the scores for each tooth and I was able to understand, tooth by tooth, where there were areas to which I needed to pay better attention. Having this information didn't really cause me to change my dental habits. I was still pretty casual as to my flossing, or I was until my next visit.

I recently went to this dentist for my three-month cleaning. She once again did a probing of the pockets. Then, on a spreadsheet she printed out, I was able to see, once again tooth by tooth, which of my scores had improved and by how much (these were in green), which scores had remained the same and which scores had gone down and by how much (these were, as you'd expect, in red). I was able to see both where I'd improved and where things had worsened.

Seeing that I had made improvements (my score had gone up on about six of my teeth) and where I'd slipped a bit (my scores were lower on three teeth) was very motivating. I am much better about flossing and using my electric toothbrush. I'm working towards improving all of my scores and not having any of them in the red on my next visit.

I've no doubt you can see where I'm going with this as it relates to the work we do, right? Knowing the level of quality you're submitting, knowing where improvements have been made, and where they need to be made, is motivating and causes people to strive to make improvements.

I know this from my experiences with clients for whom we conduct periodic assessments and provide scores on proposal quality and capabilities. Those teams are always eager to learn the results of an assessment and use that information to formulate improvement initiatives.

If you're already assessing and scoring both the quality of your proposals and your capabilities, then you know how beneficial this is and you are to be commended. If you aren't conducting assessments and getting scores to help you know how you're doing and what needs to be improved, you really should consider doing so. Hey, it got me to start flossing on a regular basis!

A for Apathy, C for Creativity? - Jon

Food – the procurement, cooking and consuming thereof – is one of my abiding passions. Before my recent trip to Singapore, I therefore invested a fair amount of time researching the city's dining options.

Hawker centres, it seemed, are the city's culinary hotbed – collections of independent stalls, each specialising in a particular dish or two. The Lobby, Starwood hotels' blog, passed on an interesting perspective:

"Singapore's Ministry of Health rates restaurants on an A-D scale not on their quality but on their cleanliness. Oddly, the rating you want to watch for is C, not A, according to Serious Eats. Here's the local logic: Being generally one-man outfits, if the hawker's food were any good, he would be flat out busy taking orders, cooking, serving, collecting payment, and doling out change. Where would he find time to clean the stall to the obsessively nit-picky standards of a government official? Therefore, only nonpopular stalls with sub-par food would be able to earn an A or B grade."

I was struck by the similarity with many proposal centres. Particularly in larger organisations, it's not uncommon to find immensely detailed, finely tuned bid and proposal processes. The governance model will be clearly defined; a barrage of reviews will take place (with teams variously red, blue, orange and more); there'll be formal project management mechanisms and communications plans. Staff are trained to follow each step religiously; cohorts of administrators schedule the necessary meetings.

But the resulting proposals are dreadful – mediocre, dull, merely 'complete and compliant' rather than 'superbly articulating a compelling story'. There's no spark, no flair, no creativity; no burning desire to produce truly first-class output, no originality, no passion.

It's almost as if they're the Singaporean 'category A' stalls – sterile environments, creating dull output, providing customers with a mundane solution. They're so absorbed in the internal process that they forget to look outward, to the customer and the competition, forgetting the very purpose of the proposal centre's existence as they do.

'Getting Real About What You Can and Can't Do'. Defining Capacity and Demand - BJ

I recently responded to post on an online forum that asked:

"How do I find time to develop content for the knowledge base when I can't even keep up with the RFPs I'm working on already?"

As I stated in my response to this person's question, "As an old hand at the game of proposals I felt compelled to write. And I'd like to address your question a bit more broadly rather than strictly as an RFP machine question. (And I apologize in advance for what may become a somewhat long response)."

--

"Dear 'Buried',

In my opinion, your question deals with symptoms rather than the core/real problem. That is, it seems to me that the real problem here is your not having a clear definition of the available capacity (what the group – in this case just you – can do each day, week, month, year).

The second component of the problem, and I'm making an assumption here, is not knowing or having a view to the demand (what is required). Then add to this the need for other projects' such as knowledge base development, etc. and very quickly you are, to use your term, 'buried'.

What is needed here is for you to clearly define (and understand) what can be done with the current (finite) resources available. The equation for this is relatively simple as you say you ARE the proposal group (the same considerations apply to a group with more than one person).

How many hours are available? (And you need to be realistic/honest here. How many hours do you have available?) Take total hours you are contracted to work (typically between 40-50), subtract sick time, vacation time, training time, meeting time, other projects time (if any), etc.

Typically, this will work out to around – 20-30 hours a week and between 44-48 weeks a year or approx. 1380 total hours available (if we use 30 hours X 46 weeks.)

144

Yep – that's right. It's MUCH less than 52 X 40 or 2080 as some less informed managers tend to think. Important to note. This is based on working a full week, but NOT defining a plan that calls for overly long hours, working weekends, etc. As many have heard me state time and time again, 'It amazes me that proposal people seem to think the only way to do proposals is in crisis mode and working to unreasonable/unpredictable schedules. This just IS NOT true and should NOT be part of your plan.'

Next step – How long does the typical proposal effort take? Here too, be honest. Base this number on what you SHOULD be doing, not what you do when you 'rush one out the door'. Figure in time for pre-proposal work, qualification, planning, strategy development, content design and development, document management, reviews and approvals, production and post-proposal activities (learning reviews, etc.).

So, as an example, let's say an effort takes 10 hours. Well, based on the calculation above, you should be able to produce 138 proposals.

This then defines your 'Capacity'. You then need to look at demand. How many proposals does the company expect/need to submit? Here too – a simple equation. Total quota divided by $ value of typical 'win'. Calculated against 'Win Rate'. So, if you need to make $500K, and each deal is worth $50k, you need to win 10 deals. If your win rate is 1 in 5, you need to submit 50 proposals.

That will give you a 'realistic' view of what you can and can't do. And REAL important to bear in mind here – this is strictly the time required for developing proposals. It doesn't include time for 'projects' such as developing or maintaining a knowledge base, developing processes, training, etc.

So, there you have it. Hope that helps and please feel free to call my way if/as you wish to discuss this further!"

Show them the high-wire - Jon

Ever feel like those in positions of power in your organisation just don't 'get it' in terms of the pain factor associated with developing proposals?

145

Ever think to yourself that if those 'on high' did realise how challenging the process was – the late engagement from salespeople lacking the necessary customer insights, the difficulties in getting the right experts involved, the late nights, the lack of resources (war rooms, graphics design skills, fit-for-purpose IT kit, decent production facilities) – they'd be horrified, and would take your calls for change more seriously?

So here's an idea. Suggest to your most senior sponsor – a VP Sales, Sales Director, someone on high who's worked with you and likes you – that each senior exec on your board should personally sponsor one proposal effort in the next two months. Not necessarily those for biggest opportunities, mind – but a random cross-section, so they get to see the full picture.

Let them sit in on meetings. Copy them in on all of the relevant documents. Charge them with helping where help is needed.

Review the proposal effort with them – being sure to pinpoint anything that happened differently and better as a result of their involvement, that wouldn't be the case on a 'normal' bid.

And then get them to share their experiences with one another.

As a result, they should understand the precarious high-wire act that characterises your proposal efforts. At the least, they might start to provide you with some safety nets and a little more time for training and rehearsal. And, at best, they'll help you to find an easier way altogether to help you find altogether easier ways to navigate the path from hearing of an opportunity to submitting a first-class proposal.

Baby I'm Amazed - BJ

I recently heard a piece on the radio entitled, "I'm Still Amazed That…" This got me thinking as to what still (after more than 25 years at it) amazes me about proposals.

So here's my list. I'm still amazed that…

146

- So many sales people don't understand the value of a proposal within the selling cycle.

- More often than not, the emphasis is more on getting the document completed on time than on quality.

- So many people working within proposal support aren't even aware of, let alone are a member of, APMP.

- We're still printing so many documents as hard copies. (In my nightmares, when I reach the gates, there's a tree in charge asking me to account for my actions.)

- The cost of proposals is often seen as, "Well, let's see. There's the paper we used, the toner. And oh yeah, we bought some pizzas, didn't we?"

- With more than two million air miles under my belt, I've only had my luggage "go missing" twice and never had a bag not found and promptly delivered to me the same or next day.

- People say such nice things about the presentations Jon and I deliver.

- I get to do what I consider to be "Fun" for a living. (And yes, I do know I'm a lucky man!)

On: training

The need for proposal training – Jon

Depressing comment from Emily, a participant on today's course for proposal staff drawn from across Australia:

"On my first proposal, I cried every night".

Interesting how many people start work on proposals by being thrown in at the deep end, with no prior experience and no training. And yet Emily's first proposal would have won or lost her company a potentially important piece of business.

Those who need it most – BJ

My experience has been that those who need to make improvements most, are the least open to admitting the need or seeking help. A recent experience with workshops that Jon and I delivered highlights this.

Within this particular company there are two divisions, and we delivered the same workshop to both. One of these divisions produces proposals of a fair to good quality (based on an audit using standardized criteria), and has a win rate of about 40%.

The other division produces proposals that are very poor (based on the same audit and criteria), and their win rate is below 10%.

The group with the higher quality and win rate saw the value of conducting the workshop, had a positive attitude and an open mind, and actively participated.

And the other group? Well, you know already, right?

From the head of the group on down, they failed to recognize the need to improve the quality or win rate, questioned the need for conducting any training, and did everything possible in an attempt to not have to attend. Then, once in the workshop (yes, the powers that be got them in their seats), they were extremely negative, refused to participate, and behaved in a rude and arrogant manner.

Of course, as one would expect, the feedback from the first group stated that they got a lot out of the workshop, and early indicators show that the changes they are making are resulting in higher quality and improved win rates. And, of course, the inverse is true for the second group. They've done nothing, and if anything, things have declined further.

And the reasons for this? They are many and varied, and I dare say, not the important question. For me the more important question, and it's applicable to many situations, is how do you make sure that you are in the first group, and that you have a realistic view as to what you're doing and are looking for ways to improve?

Riding lessons - BJ

I have a motorcycle and my partner Carol and I enjoy riding it together, with me as driver and her as a passenger. Carol had owned and ridden motorcycles some 25+ years ago but, other than as a passenger she had not ridden since then.

Recently Carol decided she'd like to ride on her own again. She found and purchased a bike that suited her. Then, being the wiser of the two of us in this couple, rather than just getting on and riding again as I would have done, she enrolled in a motorcycle course.

I told her I didn't think she needed to take the course as I knew she had logged quite a few miles back in the days when she rode (she had owned 5 or 6 bikes, both street and dirt bikes, over time). She countered that she wanted a good review of the basics before riding again and offered, "And I'm sure I'll learn a few new things too."

I've been riding motorcycles for more than 40 years, since I was...well, a long time anyway. I was confident that such a course would not offer me anything.

After Carol completed the course and qualified to have 'MC' put in her license, I asked her about what was covered and what tips she'd picked up. I was surprised by how many of the concepts, techniques and tips covered in the course I had forgotten and hadn't used in a long time. I definitely would benefit from the course, even after my many years of riding.

This supports my contention that the best training focuses on the basics, as do the workshops we offer, as well as advanced techniques. It also shows that even those who have a great deal of training will benefit from a review of the basics.

In the letter which accompanied her certificate for completing the course, the company which provided the training suggested, "Please consider taking the Rider refresher course, offered each Spring to hone your riding skills after having not ridden for a while. We also offer Advanced Rider Training to further develop your skills."

While recognizing the marketing value in this, I can also see where such courses would be very worthwhile. And no doubt many proposal professionals could benefit greatly from a yearly 'tune up' and from advanced-level proposal training.

The right (rat) stuff - Jon

BJ and I are forever seeking out real-world analogies to help us to communicate various perspectives on proposal management. So, having watched the truly fabulous 'Ratatouille' last week, my mind's been hard at work...

A rat went to work as a salesperson.

Erm, maybe not.

There was this rat, see. And it decided to get a job. In procurement.

Nah, it's not quite working, is it?

If there is a parallel, it's to provoke an interesting (and perhaps slightly controversial) debate. The rat in the movie has talent: he's instinctively a great cook, with an amazing sense of smell and taste – who's then studied with a master chef. And in the proposal world, we're passionate believers in the importance and power of effective training. Surely it should be a given that everyone working on a proposal needs to receive appropriate training in the necessary skills and techniques?

Yet I'd also argue that the best proposal managers have a set of underlying competencies, without which – no matter how well they're trained – they will only ever be good, not great. And those aren't really the mechanical things covered in, say, the APMP Foundation Level syllabus (the "how and when to run a review meeting" type of topic). They're about interpersonal skills, passion, commitment, professionalism, leadership, empathy, a gift for communication, a commitment to excellence, influencing abilities – techniques which can certainly be refined, but also need to draw on some inherent deep-seated ability.

Actually, I'd go so far as to say that if you give me someone with the right fundamental competencies and mindset, I can teach them the proposal stuff – and (if their organisation has the luxury of a little time, the ability to provide mentoring, and is capable of sheltering them to an extent as they learn) turn them into a top-flight proposal professional: someone who'll be 'great'.

But if you give me someone who's been working on proposals for years, but doesn't have the 'right stuff', we'd struggle to get them much beyond 'good'. And maybe 'good' is good enough, in a lot of cases.

It's Training, not Trained - BJ

As some of our readers will be aware, one of my hobbies is training dogs. Some of you will even have met my older pooch, Jack, as he has been my co-presenter at past APMP conferences (Dallas, Texas and Boston, Massachusetts.) For those who have met him, Jack is quite a bit older, greyer in the snout and has a hip that bothers him when the weather is cold – I know Jon, just like me, right? – but he's doing fine. Thanks for asking.

Jack is a very well-behaved dog and knows many commands. When I'm out with Jack I am often complimented on how well he listens and behaves. I've become accustomed to someone complimenting me on Jack's behavior and then inevitably saying, "I wish my dog was as well behaved."

When I ask the person what kind of training their dog has received the response is almost always, "I took him to an obedience class when he was a puppy." To this response I gently say, "Expecting your dog to be trained based on attending one class, or even a couple, is like sending a child to kindergarten, never providing any more education and expecting them to be educated. Jack behaves the way he does because he has been attending training on an ongoing basis for years and I reinforce the training at every opportunity."

The same thing occurs on the ski slopes. My wife Carol and I are both avid skiers and ski instructors. This year, Carol celebrated her 40th year with the Professional Ski Instructors of America (PSIA). As you might imagine, Carol skis exceptionally well and it is not at all uncommon for someone who sees her skiing to say, "I wish I could ski like that."

When asked as to whether that person has taken lessons, the response is similar to those I get with dog training. "I took lessons when I first started" or "I took a few lessons many, many years ago." Here too, one or two lessons doesn't do a whole lot. In Carol's case, she started out with regularly scheduled lessons for the first several years. She then became an instructor and continued to take lessons on a regular basis. (In fact, she and I are required to attend training to maintain our PSIA certifications.)

The other thing Carol and I hear is, "I've been skiing for <insert number of years here>." Here too, I try to gently point out that just skiing doesn't improve one's skiing. In fact, it can result in ingraining bad habits. Improving skills requires working on specific aspects of skiing, ideally under the guidance of someone qualified to help bring about those improvements, rather than just 'free skiing'. (Working on a specific skill is referred to as 'doing drills', and it's one of Carol's favorite things to do while on the slopes. It's one of the reasons she skis so well.)

All this relates to proposals (obviously, or I wouldn't be writing about it, right?). When Jon and I ask a person in our profession about what training they've received, the responses are very similar to those I've presented. We hear, "I took a course many years ago" or "I attended my company's proposal writing course when I first joined". Attending one course is, again, like attending basic obedience or kindergarten, and then not receiving any further education.

So, dear readers, have you been trained or are you continuing to train? Do you just keep doing the work or do you 'do drills' and work on specific areas of proposal development? Improving proposal skills and knowledge requires continual training and running drills.

The best coaching - ever! - Jon

It was great to see the list of winners of APMP's '40 under 40' awards this week - recognising some of the most talented younger people in our profession (and making me feel old in the process!). Particularly, I was delighted that our very own Kim Panesar – graphic design manager for Strategic Proposals in the UK – made the list. Much deserved!

So too did other friends, including several people I've had the pleasure of training and supporting over the years. And it made me stop and think about the two most powerful coaching interventions I had in the early days of my own career.

The first came from a negotiation guru, back in my procurement days at Barclays Bank. All of the buyers were tasked with preparing a half hour presentation about an upcoming negotiation with a vendor. Mine was packed with the latest and best industry research. I looked at the detail of the current contract. I analysed spend and usage patterns. I reviewed the supplier's performance. I compared their current pricing to external benchmarking data and to deals with other vendors selling into the bank. There were tables, graphs, numbers galore.

I presented. I sat down, happily. And was asked: "What football team does their account manager support?"

To which I confessed: "I have no idea. And, what's more, I have no idea why you asked."

That led to a wonderful discussion about the importance of emotion as well as logic in influencing – and the role of relationships and trust in the buying and selling process. They're messages that have stayed with me throughout my time in bids and proposals.

A week later, the expert was back on site, coaching some of my colleagues. I slipped an envelope underneath the door of the room he was using. Inside: a plain piece of paper, on which was written simply: 'Wycombe Wanderers'!

The other game-changer came a couple of years later. I'd just moved from procurement to proposals, appointed to the management team of one of my erstwhile suppliers to "stop us losing large bids". I arrived on day one, confident and raring to go.

My new boss – the business unit director – greeted me, and apologetically observed: "I'm afraid we don't have a desk for you yet. I suggest you go and camp out in the hot desk area on the sales floor for a couple of weeks.'

Deflated, I headed upstairs to sulk. And proceeded to learn more in the next fortnight of what makes salespeople tick than I could ever have imagined.

It was only a few years later that I realised what he'd done. "Of course we had a desk," he laughed. "But it was the cheapest and best sales training I could think of for someone who'd just swapped sides from procurement."

Two questions, then:

- who do you turn to for ideas and inspiration, and to use as a sounding board?

- have you ever spent a week sitting in your procurement department, never mind sales, observing what buyers are really like?

On: inspiration from elsewhere

The Art of (Proposal) War - Jon

Next week sees the 22nd APMP annual conference, taking place in Denver. I'm particularly looking forward to the event, as it marks the tenth consecutive year at which I'll have presented at the conference – a record for a presenter based outside the US, I would strongly suspect.

This year's theme, "The Art of Winning", takes its inspiration from Sun Tzu's famous book on military tactics, 'The Art of War', written some 2,500 years or so ago. Much as Machiavelli is my preferred evil source of reference for running proposals, it's been great fun returning to Sun Tzu's book having not read it for many years.

I thought you might enjoy a few selected quotes, which seem particularly pertinent to those of us who write proposals.

1 "Do not make war unless victory may be gained thereby; if there be prospect of victory, move; if there be no prospect, do not move." (Qualify, folks!)

2 "To be late, and hurrying to advance to meet the foe, is exhausting." (Pre-proposal planning matters: let's plan for success rather than merely responding to RFPs)

3 "These things must be known by the leader: to know them is to conquer; to know them not is to be defeated." (How clear are you with your sales teams on the information they need to dig out before you start work on a proposal?)

4 "The army that conquers makes certain of victory, and then seeks battle. The army destined to defeat, fights trusting that chance may bring success to its arms." (What a fabulous endorsement of the need to work out your proposal strategy before you start to write)

5 "If a victory be gained by a certain stratagem, do not repeat it. Vary the stratagem according to the circumstances." (We need a specific strategy for

155

every opportunity – and simply cutting and pasting the Exec Summary from the last deal isn't good enough!)

6 "The wise man considers well both advantage and disadvantage. He sees a way out of adversity." (That's why the APMP accreditation syllabus puts so much emphasis on the Bidders' Comparison Matrix)

7 "In general, the procedure of war is: the Leader, having received orders from his lord, assembles the armies." (Hey, we're working for the sales organisation, right – supporting them as they seek to win business. To an extent, we need to know our place)

8 "As a rule, the soldiers prefer high ground to low. They prefer sunny places to those the sun does not reach." (Yep, motivating the team's pretty important)

9 "Universal courage and unity depend on good management." (Ever seen a dysfunctional proposal team, with everyone pulling in opposite directions…?!)

10 "We create a situation which promises victory; but as the moment and method cannot be fixed beforehand, the plan must be modified according to the circumstances." (How relevant to the ever-changing world of managing proposals)

11 "If victory be certain from the military standpoint, fight, even if the lord forbid. If defeat be certain from the military standpoint, do not fight, even though the lord commands it." (A controversial one, this – does it encourage rogue bidding? Not necessarily one I'd want to share with salespeople, but an interesting insight into their mindset!)

12 "As has been said: 'Know thyself; know the enemy; fear not for victory.'" (That's proposal strategy in a nutshell!)

13 "To fight and conquer one hundred times is not the perfection of attainment, for the supreme art is to subdue the enemy without fighting." (Hey, if we can avoid getting into a competitive tendering process in the first place – writing pro-active proposals, especially seeking to renew existing contracts, then so much the better)

14 "He who does not employ a guide, cannot gain advantage from the ground." (Training for all participants; coaching; mentoring – all key to success)

--

It promises to be a great conference: if you're lucky enough to be attending, do come and say hi!

Learning from Seb Coe - Jon

Flying out to New York yesterday to meet up with BJ, I read the newly published autobiography of [Lord] Sebastian Coe, the record-breaking medal-winning athlete who went on to chair the London 2012 Olympic bid and project so brilliantly.

A few quotes caught my eye, that seem relevant to proposal folks:

- "Raw talent will only take you so far, and moving beyond it is never going to be comfortable." It is sometimes difficult to persuade people of the need to change the status quo: necessary upheaval when "it's worked OK in the past" can take people out of their comfort zones.

- "Excellence doesn't come cheap." Quite – if you're serious about winning the deal, and committed to improving your proposal capabilities, that requires investment of time, energy and money.

- "It is critical in any organisation to have strong leaders who will take responsibility for the actions of anyone in the organisation and let the buck stop with them." Whether leading a proposal team, or explaining their role to an executive sponsor, or managing a proposal centre (when loyalty to and protection or defence of one's staff is so essential), this really rings true.

- Before the London 2012 presentation to the IOC: "Word had it that our rivals had been severely fazed on discovering that we'd already been in Singapore for a week. It made us look organised, planned, ready for war, which we were." Unsettling the competitors: an interesting tactic for any bid team!

- On his own part in the bid presentation: "If there is one word in those five minutes that any other bid leader can say, then I'm not nailing this properly". 'Me too' is too common in many proposals and ensuing presentations.

If magazine editors did proposals... - Jon

I've had plenty of stimulating discussions recently with Mark Jones, a good friend who's helped us coach various clients over the years to write more competently and confidently.

Now, Mark's background is in journalism (he's a former features editor of the London Evening Standard) and magazine editing (including publications such as Campaign and High Life). He and I fell into conversation about the way in which a magazine editor would approach developing a publication – and the similarities and differences to the way proposals are pulled together.

As a result, he and I ran a short workshop in September for a few senior proposal folks in the UK. I scribbled down some of Mark's words of wisdom, and thought you might enjoy them:

- magazines have around five seconds to catch your attention on the newsstand: does your proposal catch the evaluator's eye in the same way?

- the importance of strong "cover lines" for a magazine to sell itself to potential readers: could we do the same with proposals?

- playing with formats – many magazines have shrunk in recent years; could that help your proposal to be different and appealing?

- the use of a "magazine within a magazine", or pull-out section, to cover specific topics

- the use of bylines (articles generally being by a named author – whereas proposal text comes from the corporation, not the individuals who would own a particular aspect of the solution: "let's hear from your people")

- the importance of design: "There's always relief for the eye somewhere on the page", and the editor and art director work closely alongside each other

- the need to make an impact from the start: the first double-page spread is usually the most expensive for advertisers, yet the opening pages of most proposals look "very dull"

- "the beginning should be big" for every article

- the use of signposts throughout the magazine ("The highlights", "Need to know", "Boring but important")

- "get the newsroom atmosphere going somehow... there's no substitute for getting people together to knock ideas around"

- "we sometimes spend more time writing the summary of the article than we do writing the article itself"

- the concept of the magazine editor "commissioning" content from writers ("who could write this best?" and "how to fit the right writer with the right story")

- "people are so sensitive about their writing"

your proposal is "like a medieval knight, flying the colours" of your organisation

- the importance of reader research (and the fine art of doing this) – "describe in three words what you felt about our proposal"; "which of the following words would you use to describe our proposal".

The church of proposal excellence

At APMP's Savannah annual conference in 2007, BJ and Jon gave the closing keynote – a spoof (but not irreverent) 'church' service. Here's an extract!

Proposal Hell

When you wouldn't choose your proposal if you were the customer...

When you hear that you've lost a deal, and can honestly say, "We knew we were never going to win"...

When a salesperson arrives with an RFP on Friday, tells you that the proposal has to be in on Monday... and thinks that's OK...

When the only graphic in your proposal is your organisation's logo on the front cover...

When the Managing Director contributes great new ideas for inclusion in the proposal... just as you're leaving the office to deliver it to the customer...

When the scariest moment of the bid is the phone call from the customer congratulating you on winning, and you realise you have to deliver that stuff that you made up at two in the morning...

When the most important professional qualification to do your job is a Masters in Photocopier Engineering...

When the Learning Review turns into an Inquest...

When your proposals happen like that because "that's the way we've always done things here"...

When your proposal process has 95 clearly documented steps, yet you typically only have three working days to respond...

When the only things that are consistent from one deal to the next are the sense of dread and the feeling of chaos...

When the longest-serving team member shown on your organisation chart is "Vacancy"...

When the only happy person you meet during the proposal project is the assistant taking your credit card at Kinko's...

When your work/life balance doesn't...

When they are surprised to learn that the software you just bought for pre-written content won't write the text all by itself...

When your pre-written content last got updated back in December, because you've all been too busy with live deals...

When your War Room is a sofa in the corner of the nearest Starbucks...

When "That will have to do" is the norm... and no-one seems to care...

When you're winning deals in spite of your proposals, not thanks to them...

... then, dear friend, you are living in proposal hell!

The fairytale proposal

Phoenix, 2005. Jon tells a specially written children's fairy story, while BJ's slides share the parallel tale of a floundering proposal support function. The kid's bit was great fun for us to write, so here goes...

--

Boys and girls, you know how fairytales work. The good guys, the bad guys, the magic – part entertainment for children, but also serving as a not-so-very-subtle morality tale.

So here's our fairy story. Are you sitting comfortably, children? Then we'll begin!

Once upon a time...

A long, long time ago, far, far away from here...

The castle

There was a fabulous castle, as grand as grand can be. There was a moat with a drawbridge, a gatehouse, turrets, and lots of those "don't even think of attacking me" type fortifications you'd expect to see on a grand, old castle.

It stood in the middle of a great, dark forest, hidden away, reached only down long, secret, shady tracks – and protected by a horde of fearsome dragons.

And in the castle lived the Queen of a rich and prosperous land.

And the Queen was beautiful and kind and generous, and much-beloved by her people.

She wore garments made of the finest silks. Her apartments were decorated with magnificent rugs from the bazaars of Atlantis, and precious tapestries carried all the way from Timbuktu. Now the Queen liked to spend her time meeting important visitors, and impressing them with her ever-increasing prosperity. So she gave great banquets, and travelled far and wide, so she could be seen by as many of her loyal subjects as possible.

162

Of course, the Queen was so busy that she had no time to actually run the country herself. Instead, she left that to her sons and daughters.

Now although the Queen was beautiful, and clever, and kind, there was one of her sons who was particularly nasty. This Evil Prince, whose name was Sir Richard, was feared throughout the land – the sort of man who chopped off the heads of a few of his enemies every year, just because…well, just because he was that sort of man, and just because he could.

So that the Queen could spend her time in banquets, and meeting people, and generally having a good time like a Queen should, the Evil Prince was given two important roles.

First, he had to make sure that enough pieces of gold were brought into the royal palace each year to pay for its upkeep. And secondly, he was responsible for all of the Royal proclamations – the announcements of new laws and new regulations that the Queen wanted to impose on her people.

Now, of course, the Evil Prince couldn't deliver all of the proclamations himself. The country was far too big, and to travel to every little hamlet would take months or years. So he had a group of servants called the Royal Announcement Team, or RATs for short, whose job it was to tour around visiting every nook and cranny of the empire. They went from village to village, gathering the loyal subjects together to present the Queen's latest announcements.

Although their travels took them far and wide, the members of the Royal Announcement Team lived a generally comfortable and indulged life. And all of the other palace servants shook their heads at quite how many pieces of gold these RATs were paid.

The hard-working scribes

So picture the scene. A member of the Royal Announcement Team stands in front of the villagers; there's an important message from the Queen.

But what if the RAT gets it wrong? What if he tells them the wrong thing? Well, that could never happen. For back in the castle, there toiled a worthy group of

Scribes, whose task it was to transcribe the royal pronouncements onto parchment, ready for the RATs to read out.

Now then, boys and girls. Let's go and visit the scribes. Come with me! Hold my hand, as we head off down the deepest, darkest, dingiest corridors in the whole castle! Beware of the bats! Brush aside the cobwebs, light your brightest candles, for few people ever venture into the Scribes' Quarters – especially children, for we all know how tasty little children can be for the sort of monsters who hide in the depths of scary Castles.

There was a Chief Scribe, who led the group, and a team of Junior Scribes, who actually did all of the hard work. And the Scribes' names were Sam, and Polly, and Lucy and Jack and Carl and Terry and Vacancy. No-one had ever actually met Vacancy, but the Chief Scribe assured them that this mysterious team member would turn up to join them one day soon.

They worked in a small room, piled high with all manner of material. There were new parchments, waiting to be written on. There were half-written parchments, still being completed. Indeed, occasionally a Scribe was found sound asleep under a stack of scrolls.

Bottles of ink, piles of quills; the scribes crowded together, shoulder to shoulder, no room to move around. And the floor was littered with rubbish – old scrolls, abandoned because of mistakes; remains of old dinners cooked for them late at night by the castle cook, McDonald.

And in the midst of this chaos, the scribes toiled ceaselessly to produce the neatest, the best-presented scrolls that anyone could ever wish to see.

No-one knew quite how the scribes were selected for their jobs: goodness knows, most five-year-olds in the country wanted to grow up to race dragons for a living, not to craft documents for the Evil Prince. There were those who whispered about past misdeeds that had led these poor unfortunates to have been sent to join the Scribes' team – and although the rumour was untrue, it sometimes felt to the scribes themselves as if that must be the case.

For theirs was not an easy life. They worked late into the night, and went home exhausted, knowing there'd be more of the same the next day. One of the younger members of the team had even been heard to ask the Head Scribe:

"Why can't we ever go home in daylight like everyone else?" But there were too many proclamations handed through their door to be written onto scrolls, and too few hours in the day for too few staff.

And although they got by – just – things seemed to only get worse. "More proclamations, less time, better quality", "More proclamations, less time, better quality" came the continuing refrain from the Evil Prince.

And when two of the team left – some say, driven insane – they weren't replaced: "You'll get more staff next year, you have my word," grinned the Evil Prince. But the next year came, and there always seemed to be other priorities in the castle – more stable hands, more cooks, more RATs.

All in all, their lot was not a happy one.

The rush job

But misfortune grew on misfortune for the team, and soon a major crisis loomed.

One day, the Evil Prince appeared at the door of the Scribes' Quarters, with an impatient look on his face. "I want a new proclamation writing up, and I want it done NOW," he growled.

"But Sir," the Chief Scribe replied, "that will scarcely be possible. We're buried in work, trying to write up the announcements you asked us for last week, and we'll be lucky if we finish those in the next three weeks."

"It's urgent. It's Her Majesty's message to her people, increasing taxes to pay for the running costs of the castle," he announced, gruffly. He paused for a minute, reflecting to himself, "You know, I did mean to warn them about this last week. Oh well, never mind." He seized the Chief Scribe by the collar. "It's important. Work nights!"

But we're already working 24-hour days, Sir."

"Then work 26-hour days, fool! Do everything you can to make sure this gets out on time. No excuses."

"But if we work any faster, we'll make mistakes," whimpered the Chief Scribe. "One little mistake and the whole parchment has to be re-written, your Highness. This is painstaking work."

The Evil Prince drew himself up to his full height and bellowed. "Painstaking work? It'll painful for you if there are any mistakes. 26-hour days it is, and no complaints. Anyway," he snarled. "How difficult can it be? It's just a few squiggles on a few pieces of old goat. Child's play. Anyone could do it. And as long as the stuff on tax is right, no-one worries about the rest of what you write."

So they worked, even longer hours than before, eyes hurting in the dim candle-light. Minor disagreements spilled out into open conflict, as the scribes became ever more weary. Jack, the oldest and therefore the most cynical amongst them, muttered incessantly: "It was never like this in the old days" – although they all knew, deep down, that it had always been like this, that nothing had ever changed... that nothing would ever change.

Some of the fine illustrations on the proclamation weren't quite so fine as usual. A few of their best quills snapped; their inkwells ran dry, and instead they had to use chalk from the schoolroom in the outer Courtyard of the castle.

But the document, though of somewhat dubious quality, was finished on time, to the great delight of the Evil Prince.

"Told you, fools," he shouted. "That's the last time I believe your sob stories. From now on, I expect an additional ten scrolls from you every week. And now I know you can do them in a day, I'll tell the Queen she can expect that in future."

And as the scribes looked out of the window of their quarters, a dark cloud passed in front of the moon – foreshadowing things to come...?

Could do better

The very next day, the Head Scribe – looking panicked – summoned his team to huddle close. "It's the Queen," he announced, "She's not happy."

And he unfurled a strange parchment, as the scribes looked in wonder. Despite their struggles, they'd always thought they did a good job – that their writing looked fine, that their illustrations were delicate and striking. But this…. This quite took their breath away. "It's a scroll from the neighbouring kingdom," the Head Scribe explained. "One of their princes visited our castle yesterday – and apparently he, erm, accidentally mislaid it."

There was the finery of the very scroll itself – not made from mere goatskin, like their own work. This must be… surely not? It was! Children, this proclamation was made from the skin of the finest unicorns in the land.

And the ink, gleaming from the page? Not made from crushed berries and potato juices, like their own ink, but (and I hesitate to say this, dear children) from dragon droppings, mixed with magicians' oil.

As for the calligraphy: had the finest artists in all the world worked for all the time imaginable, not even they could have produced pages of such illuminated beauty? It was surely not possible, the scribes murmured - but the evidence was there in front of them.

And while the scribes knew they were only transcribing announcements written by the powers that be, this…. No dry, dull prose here: this was a very joy to read. They could picture even the most cynical of the villagers listening to this proclamation, enraptured and enthralled.

"Well, The Queen's given us a whole week," the Head Scribe replied. "She wants our scrolls to be as fine, her pronouncements to be as impressive." He looked around, solemnly. "A week…" he murmured. "Tell me when you've all worked out how we're going to do it."

And with that, children, the Head headed off, straight to the Wizards' Well Bar, where he ordered himself a bottle of the very strongest Griffin Nectar.

Disaster strikes

And then, just when everything was going wrong – the urgent job, the scroll from the next country, came the third crisis for the team (because, after all, in fairy stories, bad things always happen in threes!).

Just a few days later, dear children, there was a flurry of activity around the palace. Trumpets sounded (du-du-du-daaa). Total commotion around the palace. And the Head Scribe found himself dragged away in chains by the castle guards, to face the Queen and the rest of her court.

The Evil Prince stepped forward, menacingly. "Tell me, scribe, what you meant by making me into a laughing stock, and humiliating Her Majesty?"

The Chief Scribe racked his brains. Laughing stock? Humiliation? What had he done? What had he said? "Your highnesses, I would never do anything that might harm you."

Sir Richard picked up a parchment from the table, and unrolled it. He showed the heading to the terrified Scribe: "Do you perhaps recognise this?"

"Yes, Sir."

"So would you be kind enough to tell me what it is?"

The Chief Scribe knew quite well what it was – it was the important document they'd had to produce in such a hurry the previous week. "It's The Queen's message to her villagers, warning them of the new taxes, Sir."

"Ah, so you acknowledge that you're to blame, then?"

"To blame for what, Sir?"

"Read the third sentence."

So he read. And re-read it. And the third time he read it, he gasped, noticing the crucial mistake: "Villagers will not be required to pay additional tax this year."

"Villagers will NOT be required to pay additional taxes, you say?"

"Y…y….yes, Sir. We did wonder about that, Sir, when we read what you sent us, Sir."

"Fool. TWELVE MONTHS before we can increase taxes."

"Sorry, Sir, you remember. We were rushed, Sir...."

"Wrong not on one copy, not on two copies. On EVERY copy read out by the RATs. Villagers everywhere dancing in delight, tributes being heaped on Her Majesty from every quarter of the country, praising her for her generosity. It's a bit late now to be sorry."

He looked the terrified clerk up and down. "Now before we decide what to do with you, let me ask you one more thing. Look closely at the scroll."

The Scribe peered carefully at the parchment, dreading lest he might find other mistakes – knowing, boys and girls, that he was already in pretty serious trouble.

"And what do you not see, Scribe?"

"Not see? I... I don't know, Sir."

"Let me give you a hint. It's big, it's red, it's mine. I get it out whenever I can, it's very impressive, and I'm very proud of it indeed."

"Errr....."

"My wax seal, fool. Where's the royal seal? All proclamations have to be stamped with my seal, before they're sent out."

"We didn't have time, Sir. You remember: you asked us to do everything we could to get it out on time. And we did stick them down with some of Hogwart's Very Best Glue... I mean, it almost looks as neat as your seal..."

As he was wont to do when he was angry, the Evil Prince drew himself up to his full height, which really was very high indeed. He looked first to the quivering servant in front of him, then to the Queen, and then to the Castle Guards, uttering the ominous phrase: "Take him away."

And the Head Scribe was never seen again... Some said he'd been banished from the Castle forever; others said that an even worse fate befell him, and he was thrown into the deepest, nastiest, most spider-infested dungeon in the oldest, crumbliest tower, to work with the other miscreants in the castle's procurement team.

The fairies arrive

When the team heard tell of their boss's terrible fate, they wept copious tears for many minutes, then started to wonder what to do.

"There are ten more proclamations coming in for us to write," one of them bemoaned.

"We only have one day left before the Queen wants to know how we'll make our scrolls better," cried another.

"The Head Scribe is gone. The Evil Prince is on the warpath," the next sobbed.

"Whatever shall we do?" they sighed in unison.

"We could take some magic mushrooms, so we don't need to sleep."

"We could poison the Queen, so she never wakes up!"

"I've got some pictures of Sir Richard doing naughty things in the stable that we could sell…"

Children, they looked at one another, and sadly shook their heads. And then the youngest member of the team piped up timidly: "But none of that will work. What are we going to do? We need a magician, or something, the state we're in…"

And Jack, who as you'll remember was the oldest and most cynical member of the team, muttered darkly from beneath his thick white beard: "Oh yeah. That'll work. Magicians. Abracadabra…" He stopped and looked around. "See… nothing. Abracadabra…. Told you…"

Do you believe in fairies, children?

Do you really? If you do, let's try one more time. Boys and girls, we want you to say it together with us: "I believe in fairies!"

Suddenly, to their amazement, there was a blinding flash of light, and there, fluttering before them, was a strange vision.

It couldn't be… it was….

There were two fairies, complete with magic wands!

"Anything we can do round here?" piped the first fairy, gruffly, as they settled down on the table in front of the incredulous scribes.

"Who on earth said abracadabra?" complained the second fairy bitterly. "I had my feet up in the bar, I did, and I'd just ordered my eight litre of beer."

The Scribes looked amazed, but before too long they were recounting their every woe to the fairies. The struggles, the trials, the tribulations. The blood, the sweat, the tears. The mounting crises.

The fairies turned to one another, and drew out a great book. They peered at its pages intently. "Remember that time across in the other kingdom?" "I do." "Bit different here, isn't it?" "Yep." "Same sort of thing, though, isn't it, basically." "It is."

"And the Queen will be happy whatever we do?" "Yeah, we'll put her under a spell. She'll do anything we want, then."

And then the fairies whispered to each other, rubbed their hands together and squealed excitedly: "OK, let's play…."

So the two fairies leapt in the air and set to work, waving their wands gaily around. They waved them at the wall, and a tap appeared. One of the scribes ran towards it, and turned it on – and a stream of golden liquid flooded out. The scribes looked closely; one dared touch it, and put her fingers to her lips. "It can't be!" "It is…dragon droppings and magician oil!"

They waved their wands outside, and a strange high-pitched neighing sound pierced the air, coming from the courtyard. The scribes rushed to the windows, peering out, as a whole pack of unicorns was ushered towards the stables. "Skins," the first fairy muttered, a little too gleefully for some.

"Stand back" the first fairy cried, as the second grabbed his wand firmly. And with a blinding flash, five strangers appeared in the midst of the scribes. One of the newcomers stepped forward: "We are in the right place, aren't we? We're the new scribes." And even more miraculously, cynical old Jack was nowhere to be seen. "Gone to work in the bakery," one of the fairies laughed, noting their excitement.

"Watch us," the fairies ordered, and every head in the room turned their way. And then... well, even years later, none of them could remember what exactly had happened. It was as if everyone in the castle had fallen into the deepest sleep – yet when they woke up, they recalled classrooms and teachers; they remembered meeting strange beings who called themselves 'Consultants'. And they found that they had suddenly mastered all of the skills needed to produce the most beautiful scrolls imaginable.

As they waived their wands, the walls of the Scribes Quarters' changed colour, now glistening with bright yellows and pinks. The space seemed to expand before their very eyes, until the Quarters were three times as big as they had been before. And even more miraculously, they were no longer hidden in the darkest recesses of the castle – the fairies had moved the Scribes' Quarters lock, stock and every smoking barrel into the nicest, most picturesque tower in the whole castle.

And finally the fairies flew out into the castle courtyard, where the Evil Prince was returning from a hunting expedition. And Sir Richard's horse reared up, stamping his hooves, and flung the Evil Prince to the ground. Children, I'll spare you the horrible details, but let's just say that he wasn't ever going to be troubling the Scribes again.

And then, giving one another a final happy embrace, and with a final wave of their wands, the fairies were gone.

Happily ever after

Children, I can only begin to tell you what happened next. The scribes went back to work, happier than ever before. Laughter echoed around the room, as they went about their work.

Everything they did worked just like magic – they only had to look at a sentence on a page, and it seemed to re-order itself and sing out its message with amazing clarity. They wrote with their new dodo-feather quills, and their letters and illustrations took on a miraculous quality. The scrolls were now made of the finest unicorn. Never again did the Queen send them proclamations to produce in less than...oh, three whole days. And they were always checked before they were sent out.

What's more, children, the Scribes managed to get to bed early every night, and some of them even went to sleep.

They became well-known for producing the best proclamations in the whole wide world. And, as you might very well expect... they all lived happily ever after.

Fifty shades of great

A certain book caught the public's imagination in 2011. At APMP's conference in Atlanta in 2013, BJ and Jon presented a spoof version. Each section of the tale generated giggles in the audience – and was mirrored by a practical plan for organisations looking to improve their proposal capabilities.

Here goes: only read on if you're open-minded and have a sense of humour!

--

Flirtation

She is a sweet young woman. Sheltered. Innocent. A virgin at the age of 21 (don't laugh). She's a student, just finishing her degree. She works part-time in a hardware store – which conveniently (it will transpire as we share her story) sells items such as masking tape, rope and cable ties.

He is a Chief Executive. Young. Dashing. Wealthy beyond belief, having built up a major conglomerate by the age of 28. (Hey, no-one said this stuff was realistic).

Little do they realise when they meet – somewhat improbably – in his luxurious penthouse office that their lives are about to change beyond all recognition.

He flirts with her, teases her, sends her improbably expensive gifts. She feels herself lured by his witty, penetrating conversation; his good lucks; his large... helicopter.

He invites her back to his place. It soon becomes clear that he wants her to join him for more than merely a cup of coffee...

1 Find a C-level executive to act as the personal sponsor & champion for your proposal function.

2 Calculate the revenue proposals generate – and the jobs they create – and promote the ROI generated by the proposal support function.

3 Calculate a realistic yet generous budget for effectively managing proposals – without cutting corners – and ensure this is under the direct, discretionary control of the head of the proposal function.

4 Create trust with sales by producing high-quality proposals – taking away the pain, and helping them to win more business.

Resources

He shows her into his so-called playroom – or, as she will later come to know it, his "red room of pain".

From the walls hang an assortment of frankly scary-looking items: paddles, whips, riding crops and 'funny-looking feathery implements'.

Her eyes are wide with surprise and excitement: she's never seen anything like it. They certainly don't have this sort of thing back home in Seattle...

5 Provide your proposal staff with a working environment conducive to effective, creative work.

6 Ensure you have ready access to war rooms for proposal development.

7 Create a comprehensive library of strategic, up-to-date, easy-to-tailor pre-written proposal content and graphics.

Contract

He asks her to sign a 'contract'. It outlines the 'rules' for their relationship; the boundaries and limits; agreements as to how they might play safely and consensually.

"He wants to do that, to me?" she wonders – breathless at the thought. After the initial shock, she begins to realise that, deep down, maybe she craves this too.

8 Define clearly the process by which your sales staff should engage the proposal support function, and the services that will (and will not) be provided.

9 Establish a clear and measurable service level agreement in place with your sales and business colleagues.

10 Build a clear capacity plan showing the number of deals your proposal centre can support, and ensure that you have the corresponding staffing level in place.

11 Help sales to write proactive proposals to retain and extend existing contracts without these going to competitive tender.

12 Coach sales to engage you as soon as an opportunity is a realistic twinkle in their eyes, so you can undertake thorough pre-proposal planning to shape the deal in your favour.

Seduction

It's clear to her that he is no ingénue. He's had numerous partners; played the field; flirted and fondled and fantasised with lots of others. But, he tells her: she is different. Special. Perhaps she's the one...

She trusts him. She wants it so badly. She lets him take her forcefully... sorry, she lets him take her forcefully to his bedroom.

Before long – and those of you of nervous disposition please cover your ears – he has her tied to the bed. He tells her clearly, explicitly, exactly what he intends to do to her.

Rude things happened.

13 Establish a robust, active qualification process in place that ensures you only work on the right deals – treating each opportunity as qualified out until it is qualified in.

14 Develop a clear, compelling strategy to seduce your client's decision-makers for each opportunity. If you don't have a compelling story to tell, don't bother!

15 Conduct a high-quality kick-off workshop to engage, inform, motivate and connect your team.

16 Design content before starting to write, working out how to maximise your scores.

Obedience

But mere frolics in the bedroom, the living room, the office, the helicopter... are not enough for his tastes. He wants more. Much more.

She is to be his; to obey him at all times, to allow him to take responsibility for her "training, guidance and discipline".

17 Document your proposal process clearly, and ensure it is understood, supported - and obeyed - by all parties.

18 Ensure that the right people are fully, quickly and willingly engaged once a deal is qualified in: proposals should be part of the role descriptions and objectives for the staff involved; insist that those taking the decision to qualify in then ensure their staff's active involvement.

19 Clearly document and explain the roles and responsibilities of all those involved in proposal development.

20 Train all those involved in proposal development in the necessary techniques.

21 Be a proposal evangelist: champion best practices throughout the business, regularly.

Discipline

They swap numerous emails: flirtatious, suggestive, downright naughty... Her heart pounds each time a message appears from him in her inbox.

She knows that he is there for her: helping her to behave in the way she wants. Supporting her. Advising her. Caring for her. Ultimately, this is as much about her needs and desires as it is about his. Yet she understands that there will be severe consequences if she fails to follow their rules.

22 Adopt a disciplined approach to developing – as opposed to merely writing – content.

23 Foster the development of proposals that are a joy to read, by editing and proofreading content so that it is high quality. Build the necessary time into your plan.

24 Use social media, as well as more traditional techniques, to share information between team members working on your proposals.

25 Establish a well-structured coaching and mentoring program for all staff in your proposal function. Mentor and / or be mentored.

26 Accredit your proposal staff – and not just to Foundation Level.

Punishment

He monitors her behaviour. She knows it is for her own good – what she wants. But she pushes boundaries, tests his authority. Breaks the agreed rules.

He looks at her disapprovingly. Explains sternly why her conduct is unacceptable. Puts her across his lap, and addresses the matter in a way she is unlikely to forget in a hurry...

27 Ensure that all strategic deals have strong and active executive sponsorship.

28 All of your proposal managers should be skilled in project management and leadership; train them to a high standard and give them the necessary authority.

29 Ensure that there are consequences for those who don't meet deadlines or who don't produce quality results.

30 Conduct reviews and approvals in accordance with a robust yet flexible governance process.

Submission

Punished, held tight: she's his girl now. Relishing what he brings to her life, emotionally and physically.

Her days become a blur of intense experiences, each different yet amazing:

31 Submit proposals that are professional in look and feel, designed in a way which brings your story to life.

32 Draw! Ensure that all of your proposals include excellent, customer-centric graphics to enliven and explain your story.

33 Don't fall behind the pack with your proposal output. (Think poster proposals, iPads, website submissions, bid portals, contemporary binding and packaging...)

34 Remember that production is best left to the experts – but only to experts who 'get' proposals.

35 Production and submission: have a Plan B...and C.

36 Consider design very early, so that your proposal documentation is consistent with other bid collateral.

Satisfaction

He knows precisely what to do: knows which of his girl's hot buttons to press. He brings her to moments of sheer ecstasy – again and again and again and again...

37 Win more.

38 Compensate your proposal staff more than adequately – salaries, bonuses, recognition, time off...

Reflection

"How was it for you?" he asks.

"Oh goodness, that was amazing," she tells him when she's finally able to recover her breath.

 "You're the best, the sexiest, the hottest man I've ever had," she tells him.

"I know: because I'm the only man you've ever had," he replies. "But I've known lots of women, and I've never met one as wonderful as you ..."

39 Conduct effective learning reviews internally, win or lose, recognising what worked well and what could have gone better.

40 Conduct effective and insightful client debriefs at the end of each bid/proposal effort, ensuring that feedback on proposal quality is specifically captured.

41 Make your executive sponsor accountable for implementing actions and sharing knowledge as a result of your learning reviews.

42 Benchmark your proposal output and capabilities objectively and independently and on a regular basis.

43 Have a client audit program in place, to regularly understand and quantify evaluators' views of the quality of your proposals compared to those of your competitors.

Commitment

And so our heroes come together... come together as a couple, sharing their lives and celebrating their now-mutual tastes for the daring, the new, the exciting – and for one another.

44 Ensure that roles in your proposal function are filled by staff committed to a career in proposal management.

45 Attending APMP events is a right, not a privilege. Make sure your senior management understand this.

46 Share knowledge between team members on a regular basis and help them to improve their skills and knowledge.

47 'Will-win' deals, not merely 'must-win'. Get serious!

48 Celebrate success.

49 Write a list of things that would make your proposal function a better place to work. And do something about them.

50 Build a clear, costed, prioritised improvement plan to enhance your proposal capabilities in the coming year; get it agreed and secure the necessary funding.

...and they all live happily ever after.

Be bold but be safe; seize opportunities to explore the new and interesting when they present themselves. Above all, don't be afraid to be yourself.

Your job? To ensure everyone in the organisation is fully committed to developing and submitting only high-quality proposals – and to doing so in an efficient manner.

Establish the rules. Gain trust and commitment. Ensure the rules are followed. Punish those who don't. Enjoy what you're doing. Submit without fear.

Keep in touch!

We both hope you've enjoying dipping into this anthology! If you've found a few things to make you smile with recognition, and taken away a few useful ideas, our job here is done.

If you'd like to read more from us, the blog's updated regularly at www.theproposalguys.com – and you can subscribe there to receive new updates by email.

You can read more about the company we lead and the wonderful team we work with at www.strategicproposals.com.

One other useful resource you might enjoy: our free online benchmarking tool at www.proposalbenchmarker.com.

And we love hearing from friends in the profession. You can contact us by email, of course (bj@strategicproposals.com and jw@strategicproposals.com), and we'd enjoy receiving your notes.

Good luck – and keep in touch!

Copyright

Printed in Great Britain
by Amazon